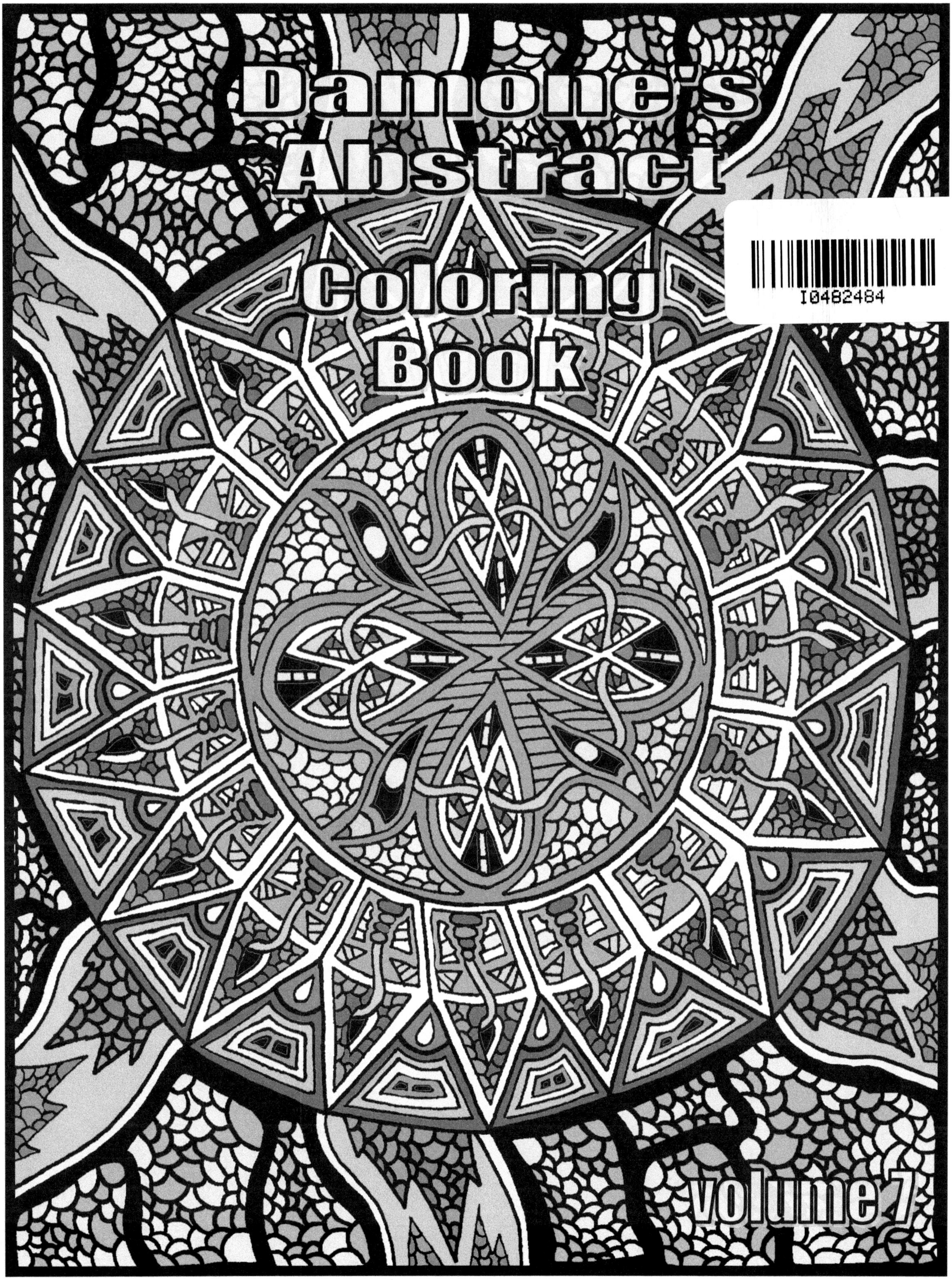
Damone's
Abstract
Coloring
Book
volume 7

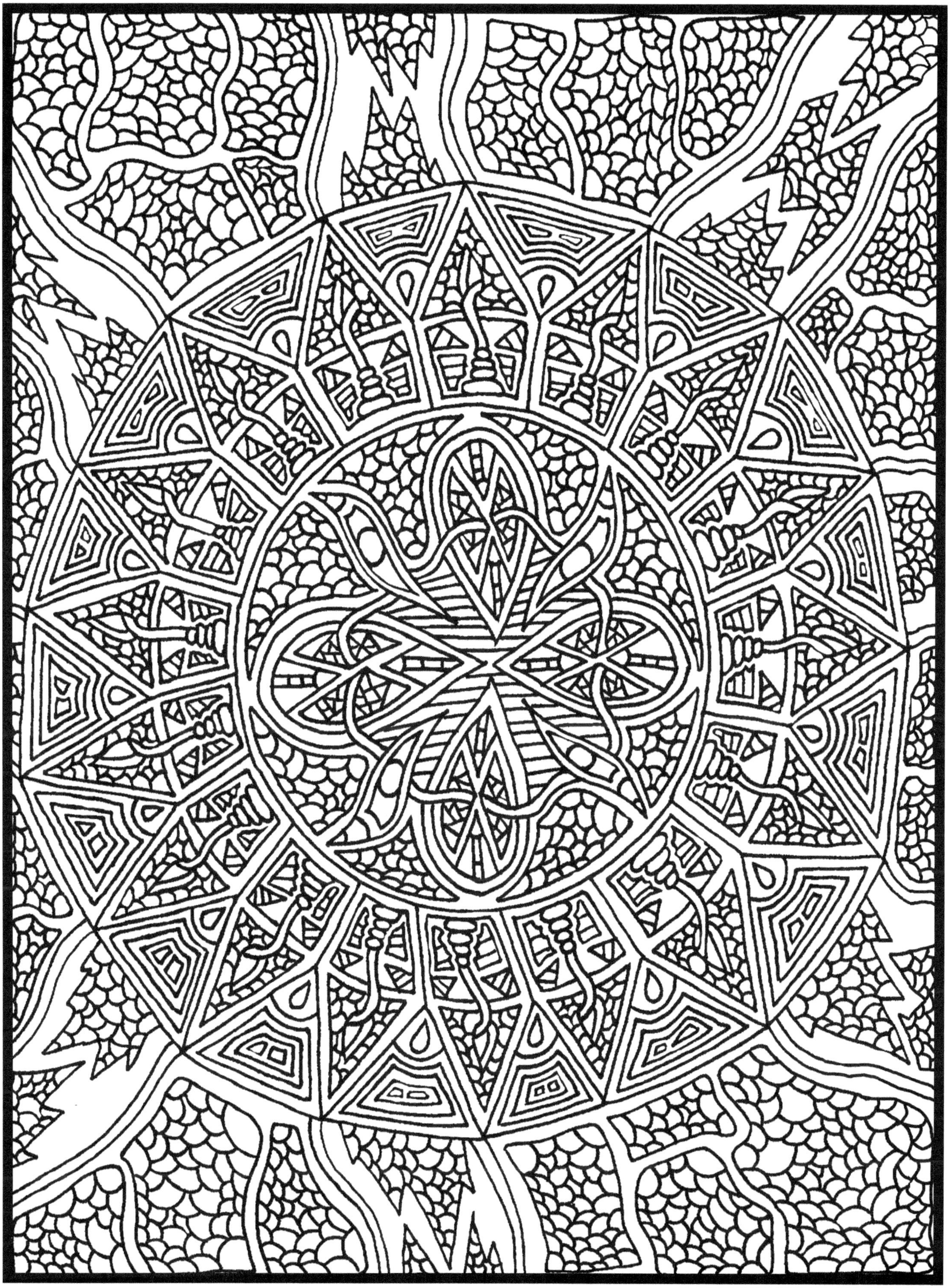

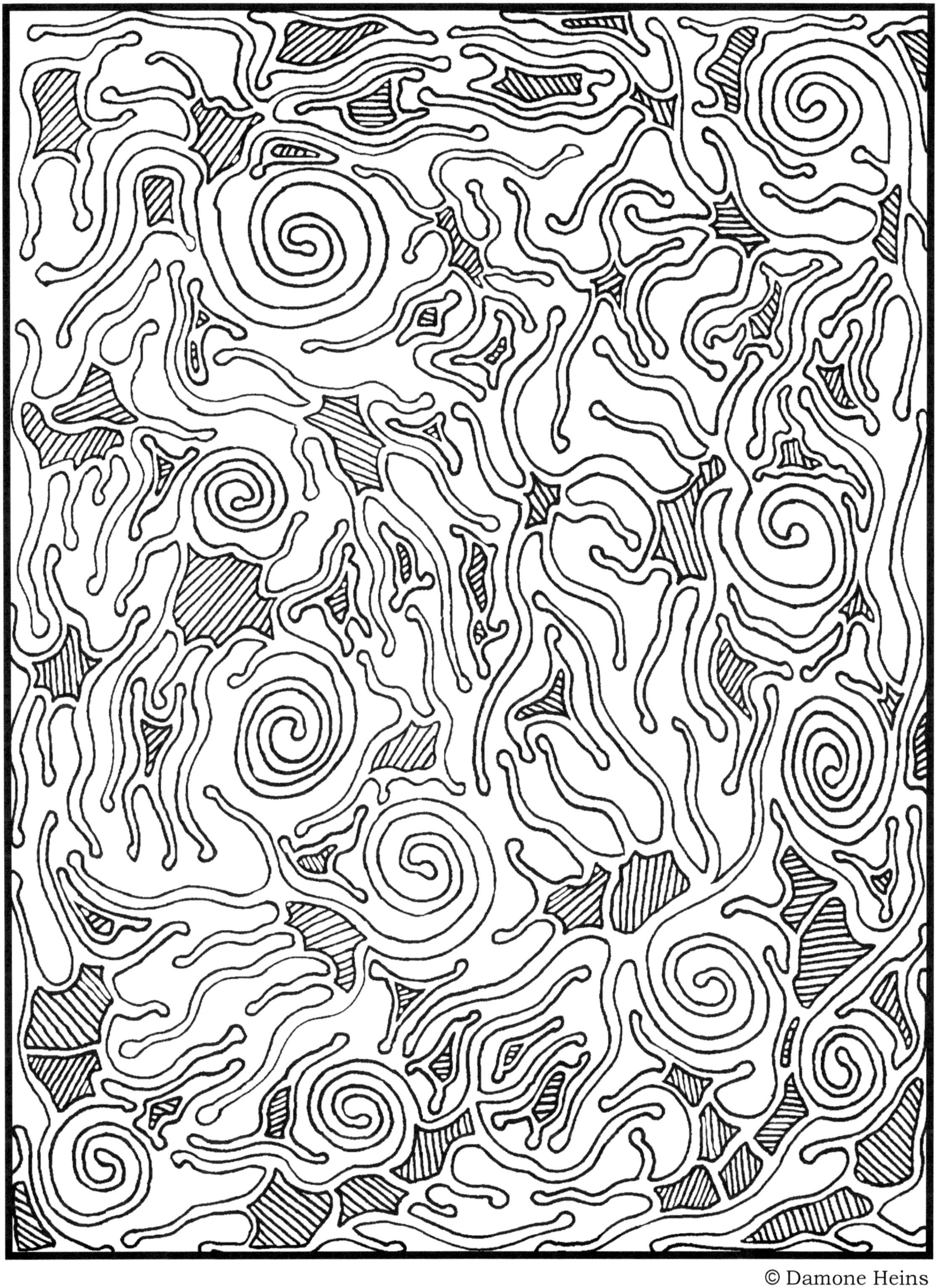

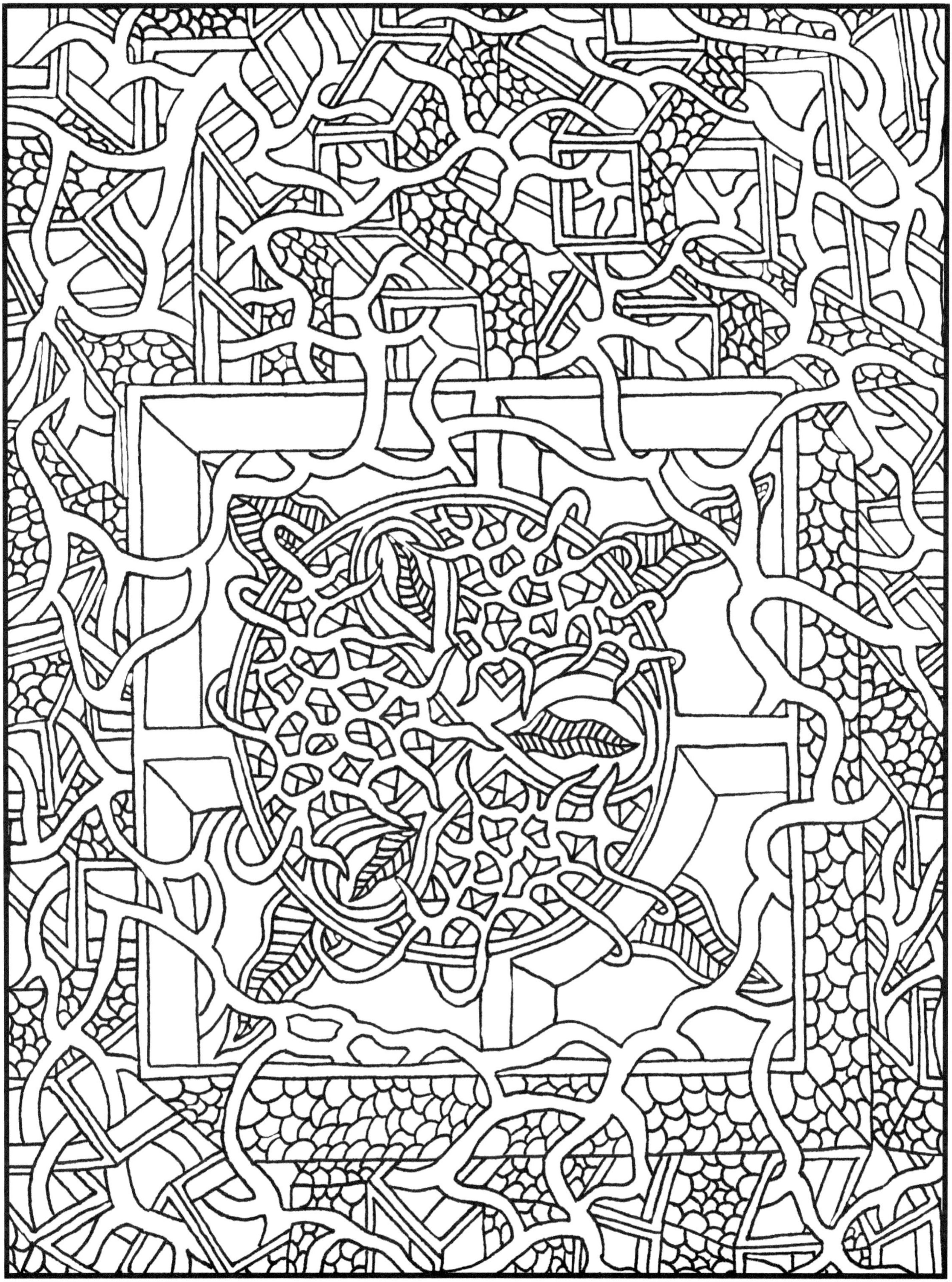

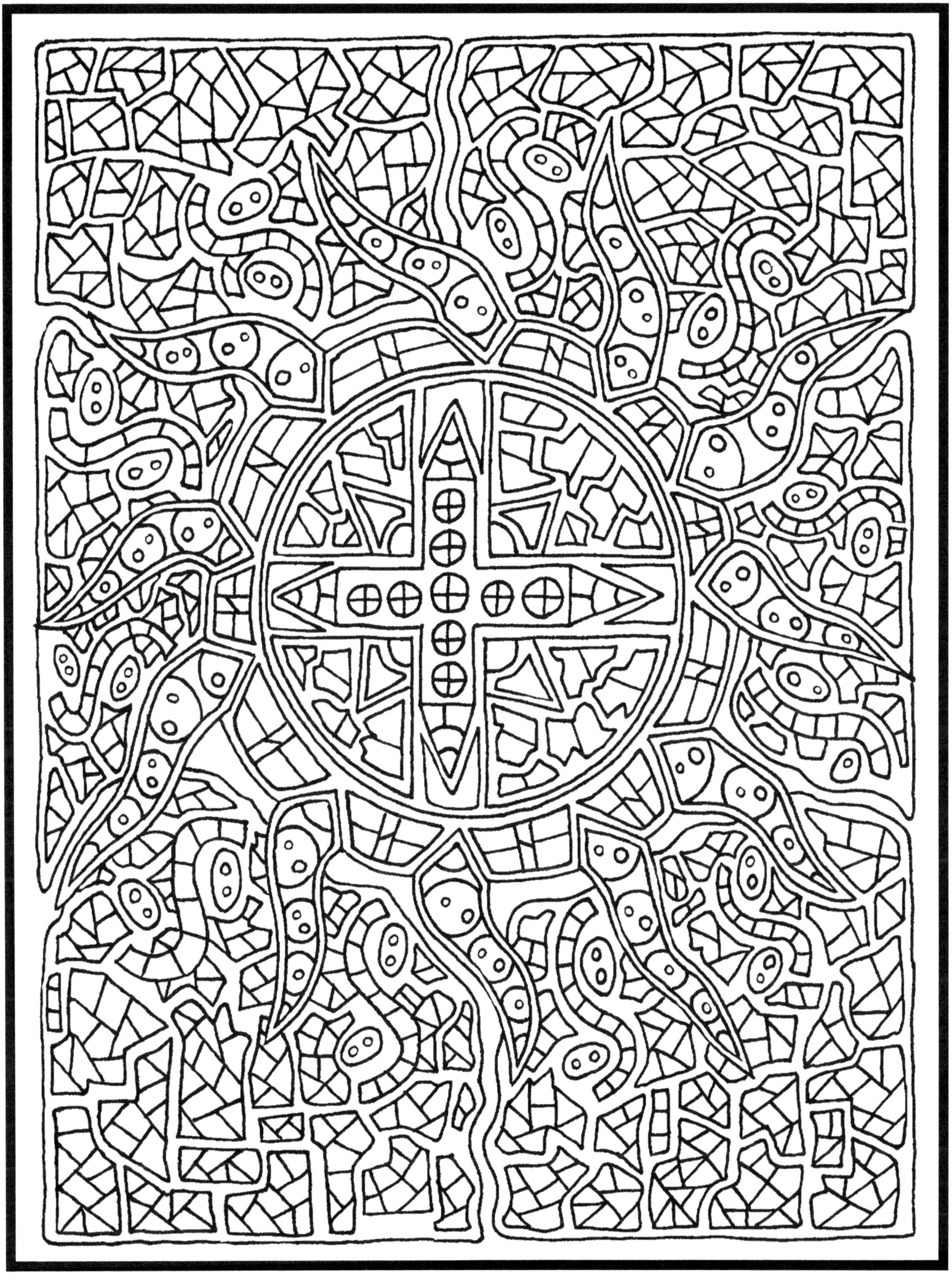

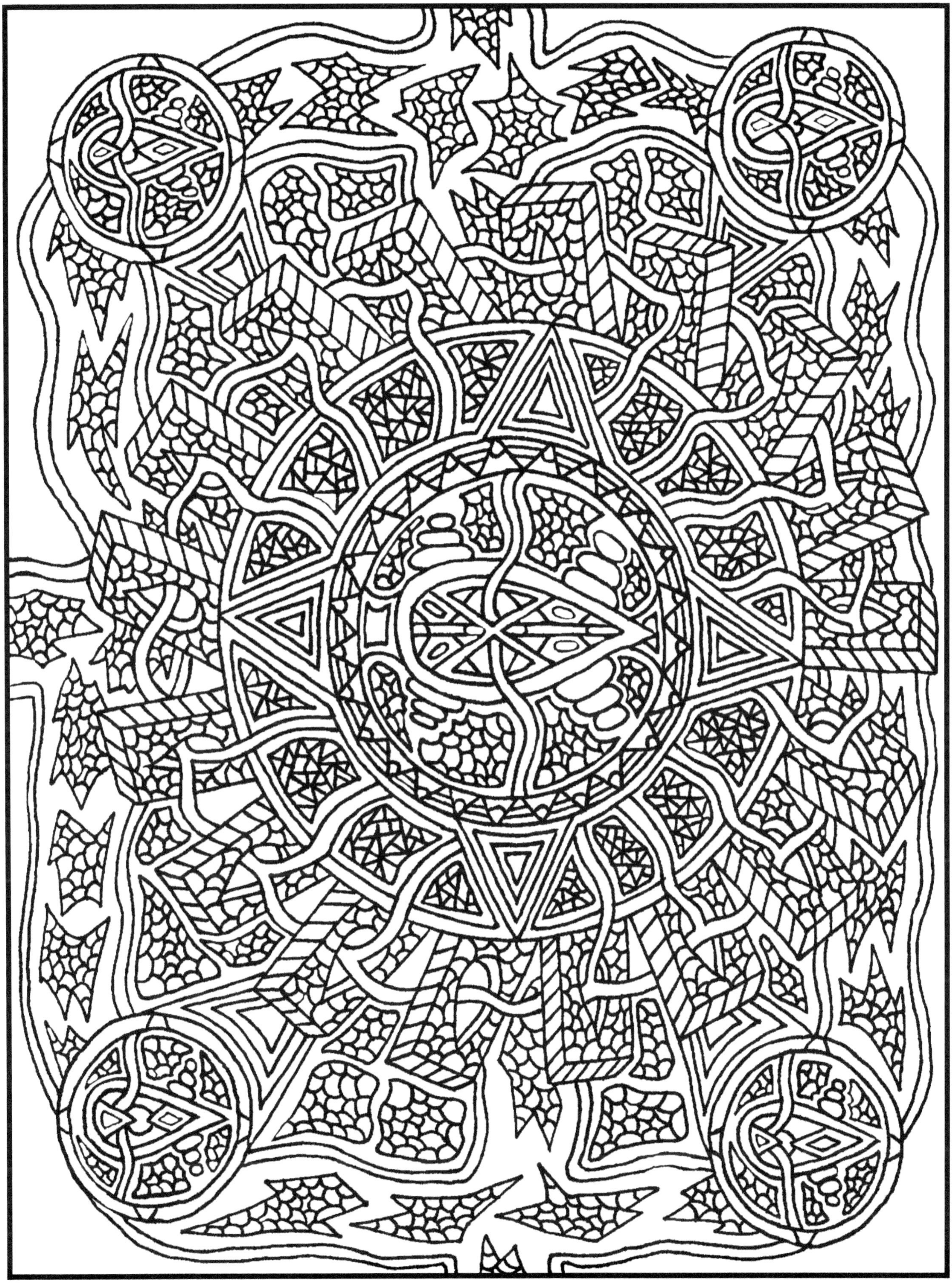

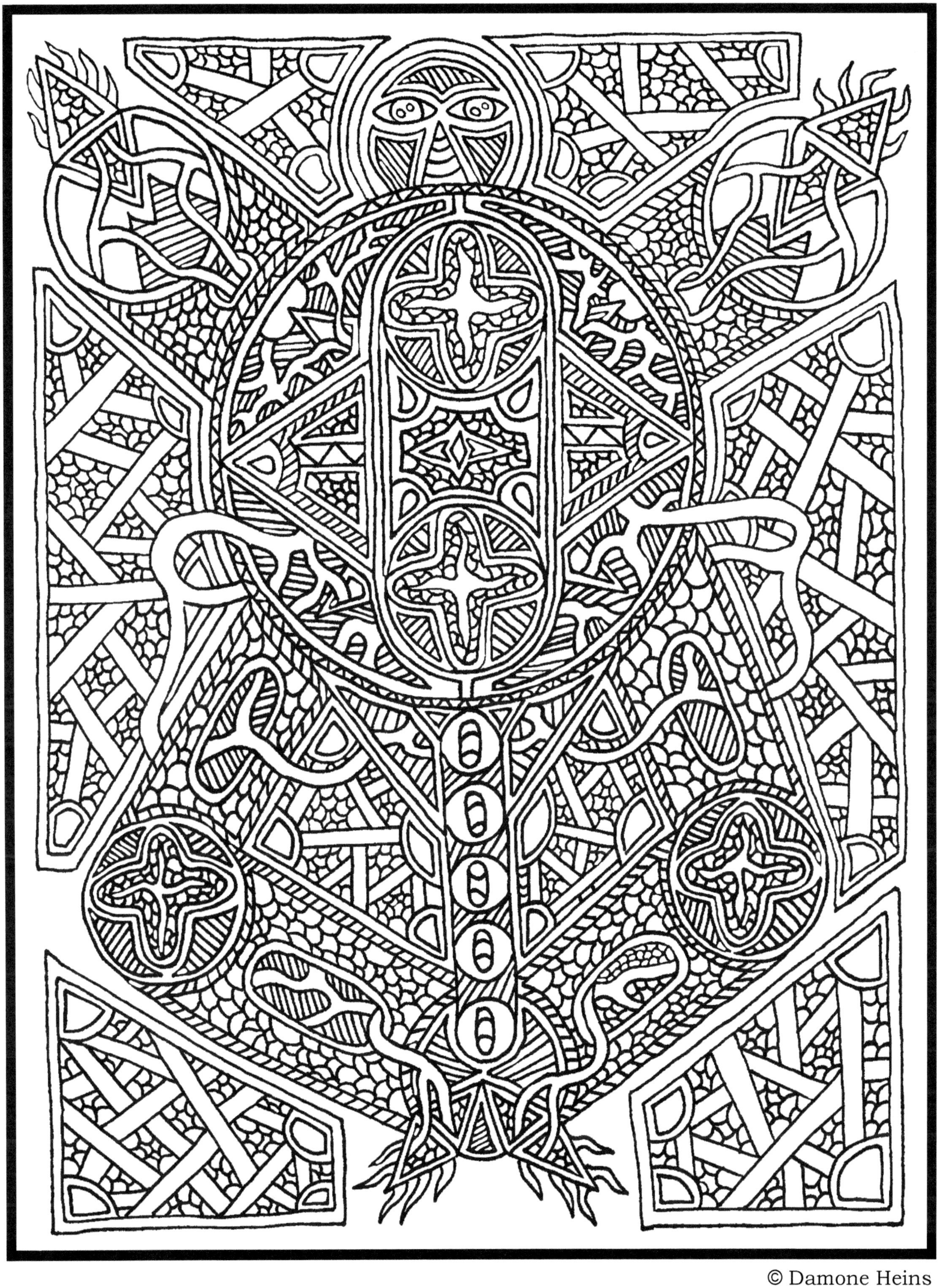

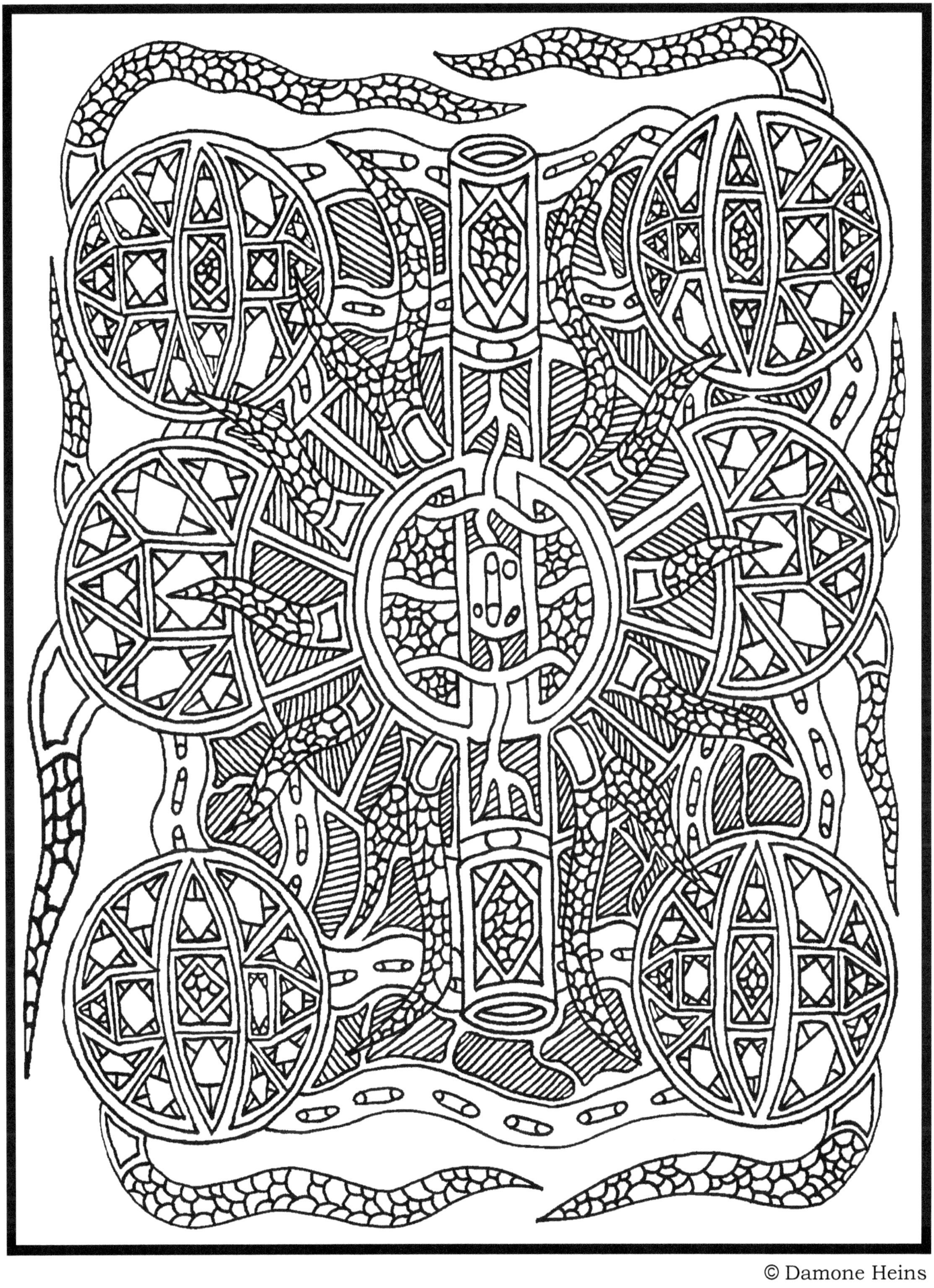

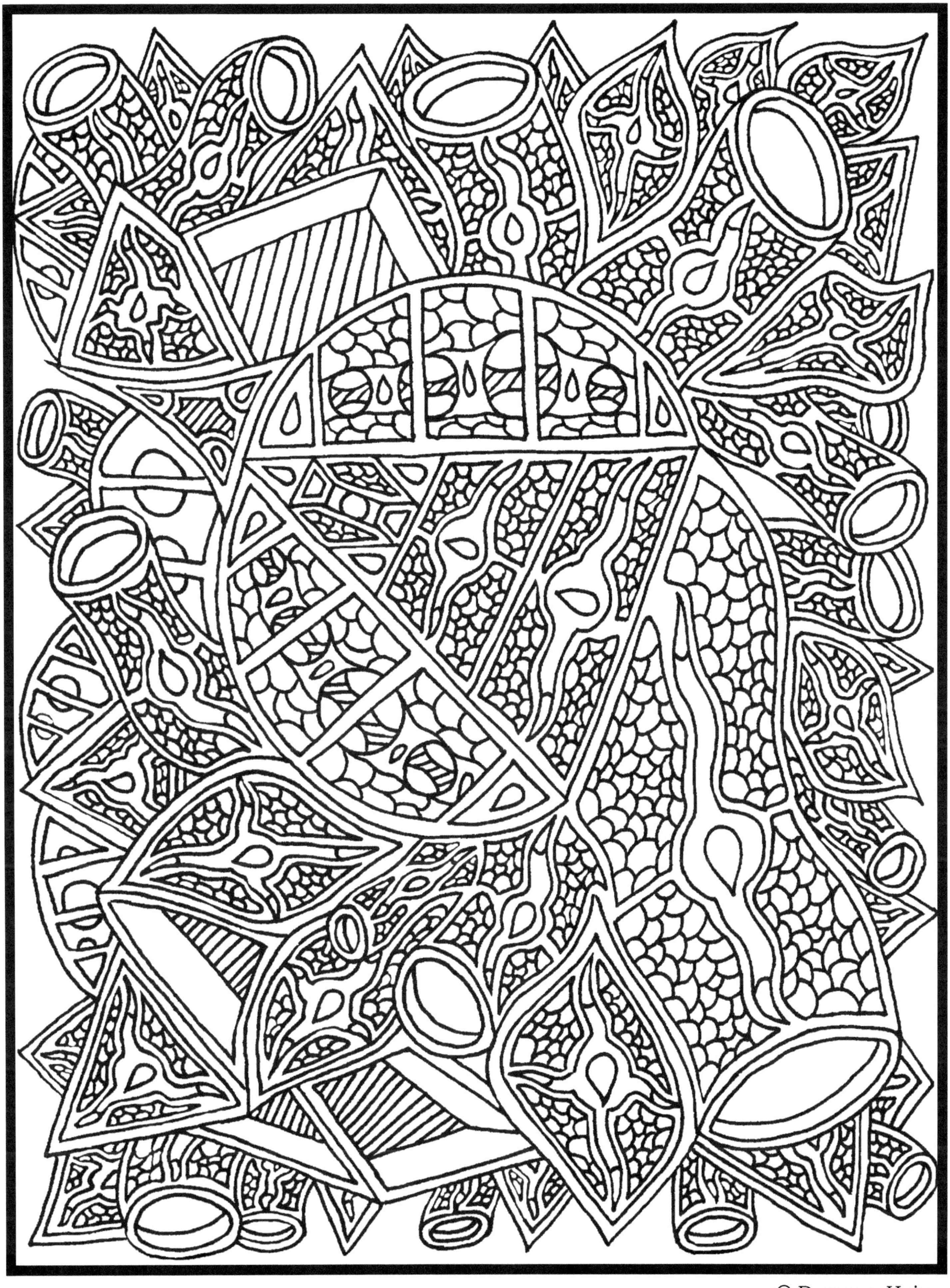

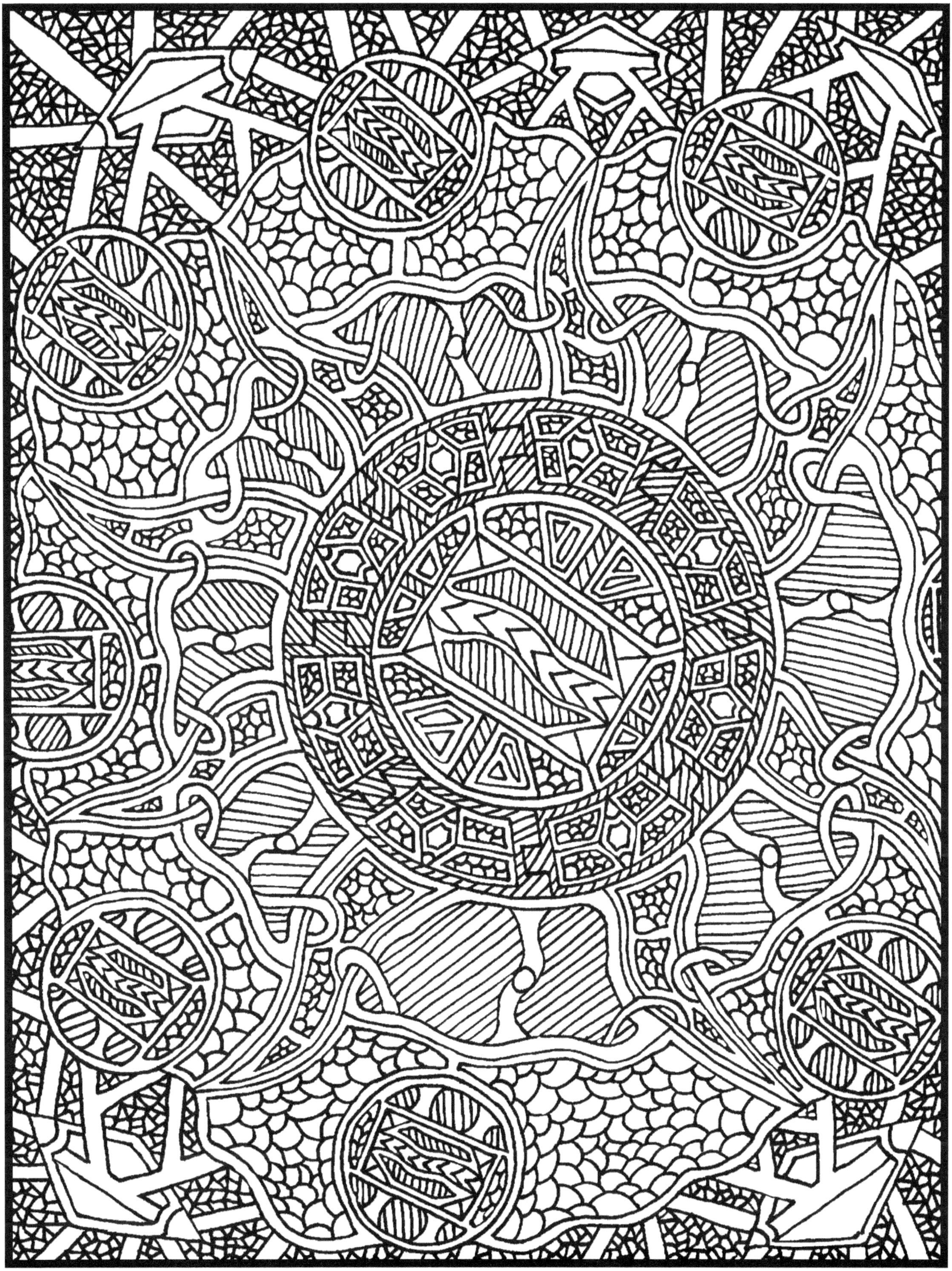

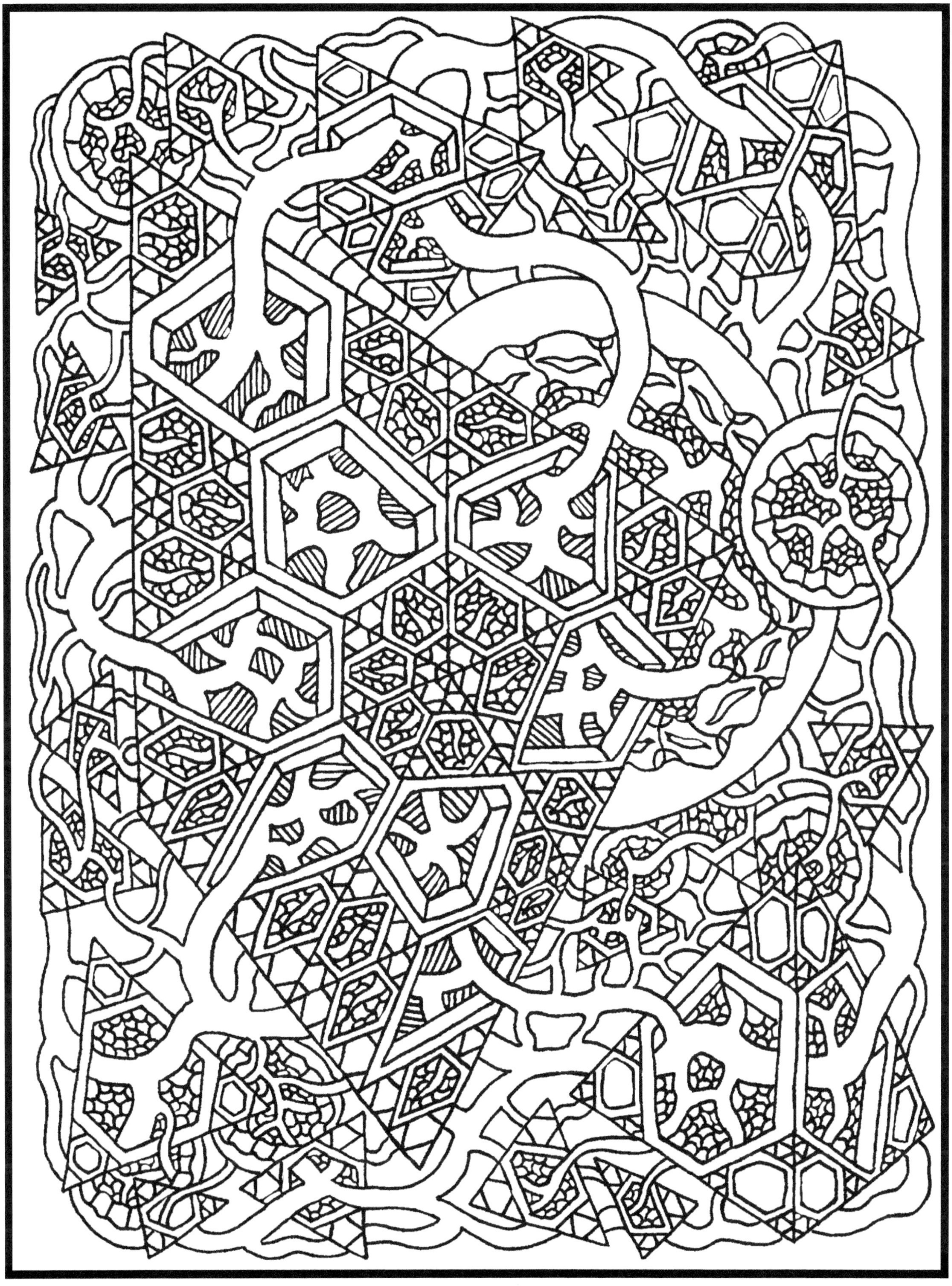

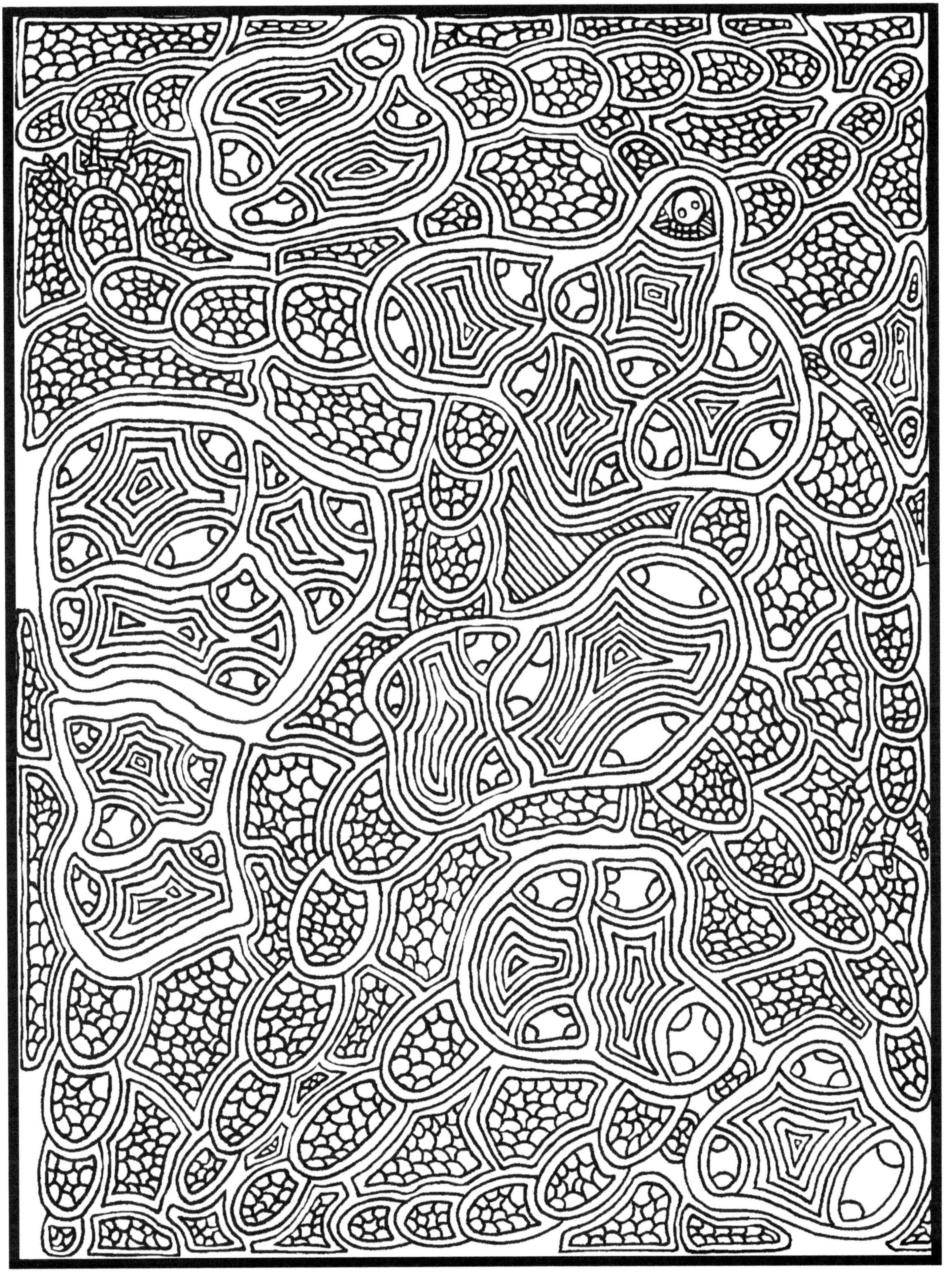

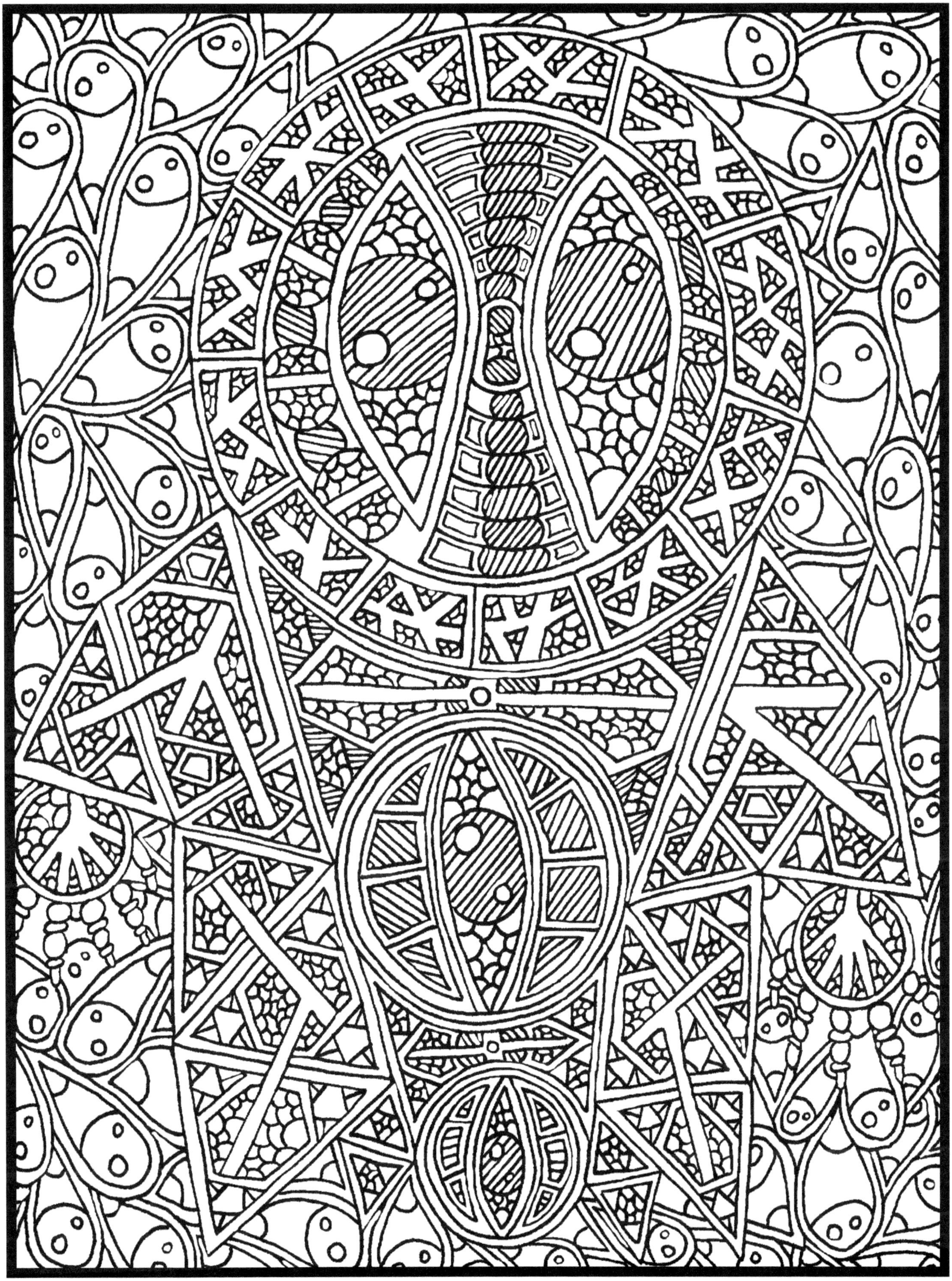

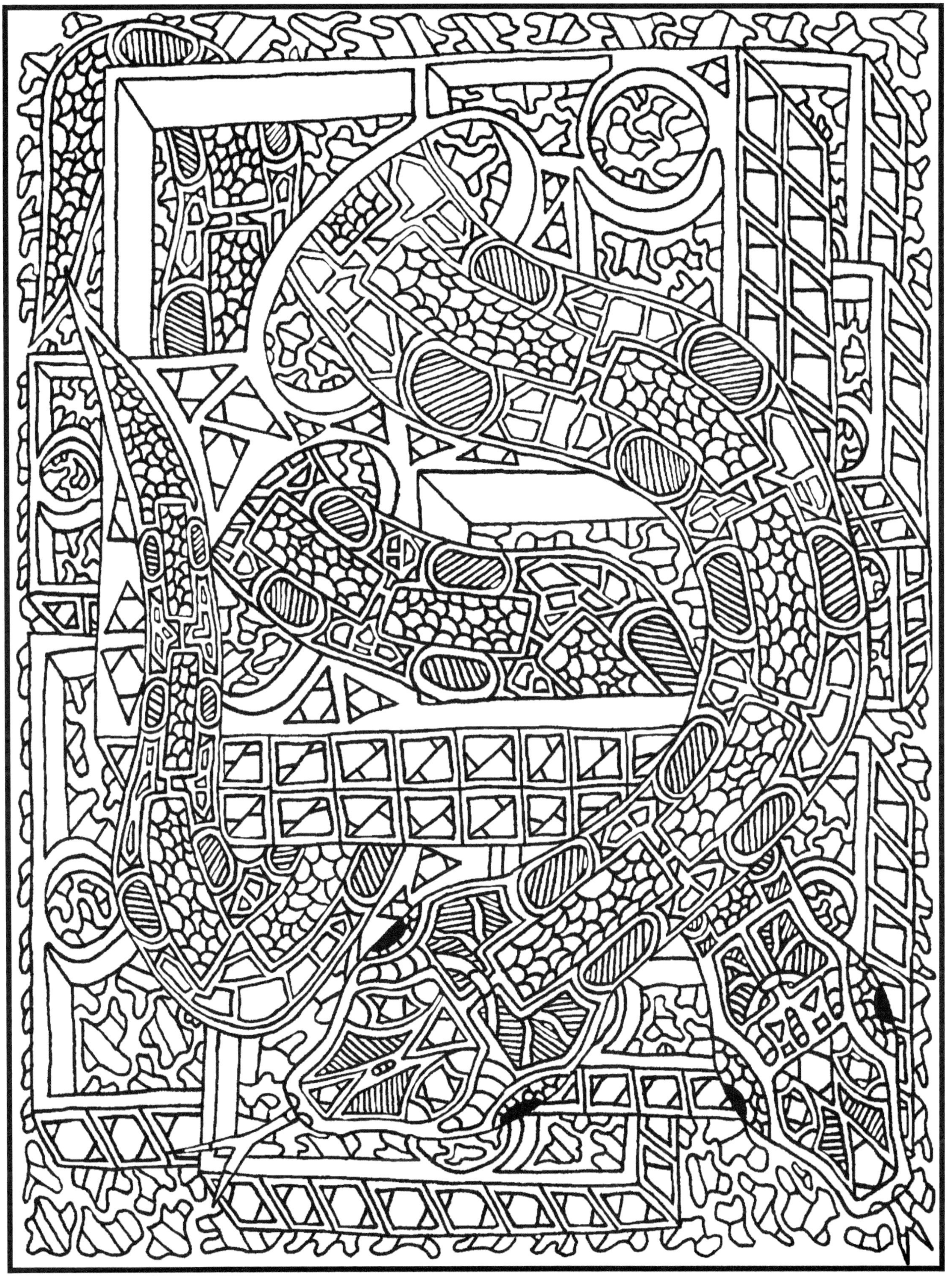

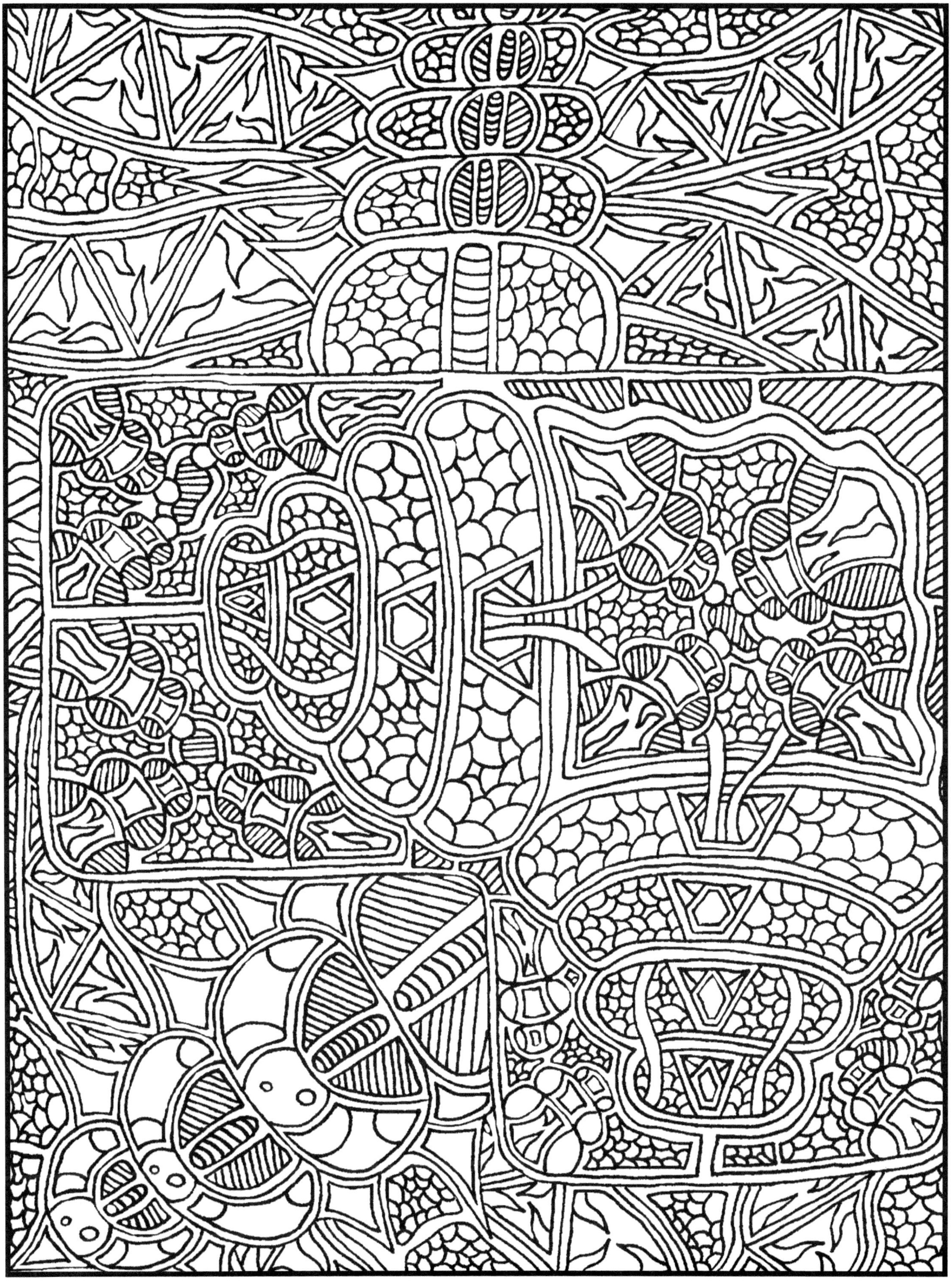

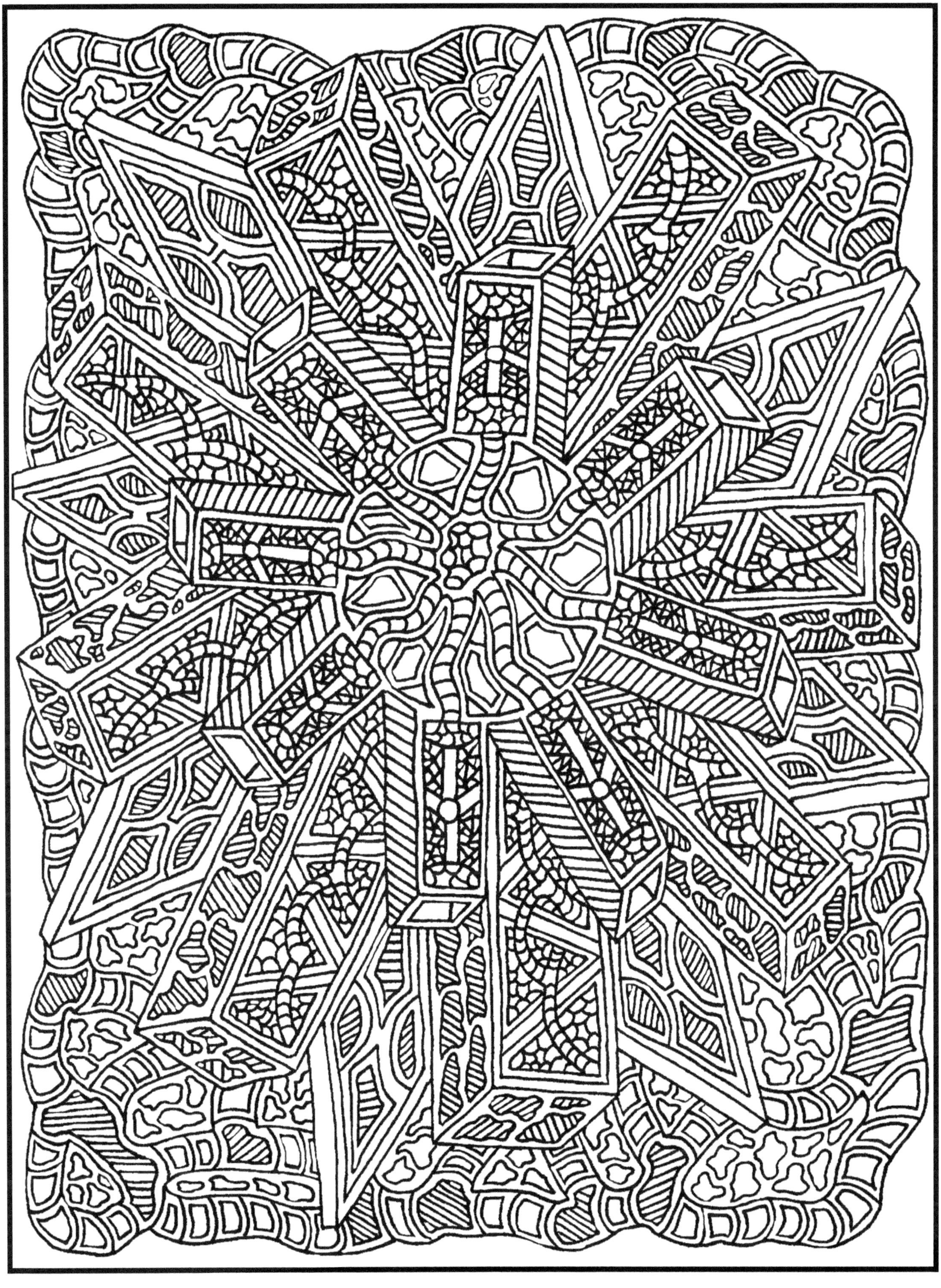

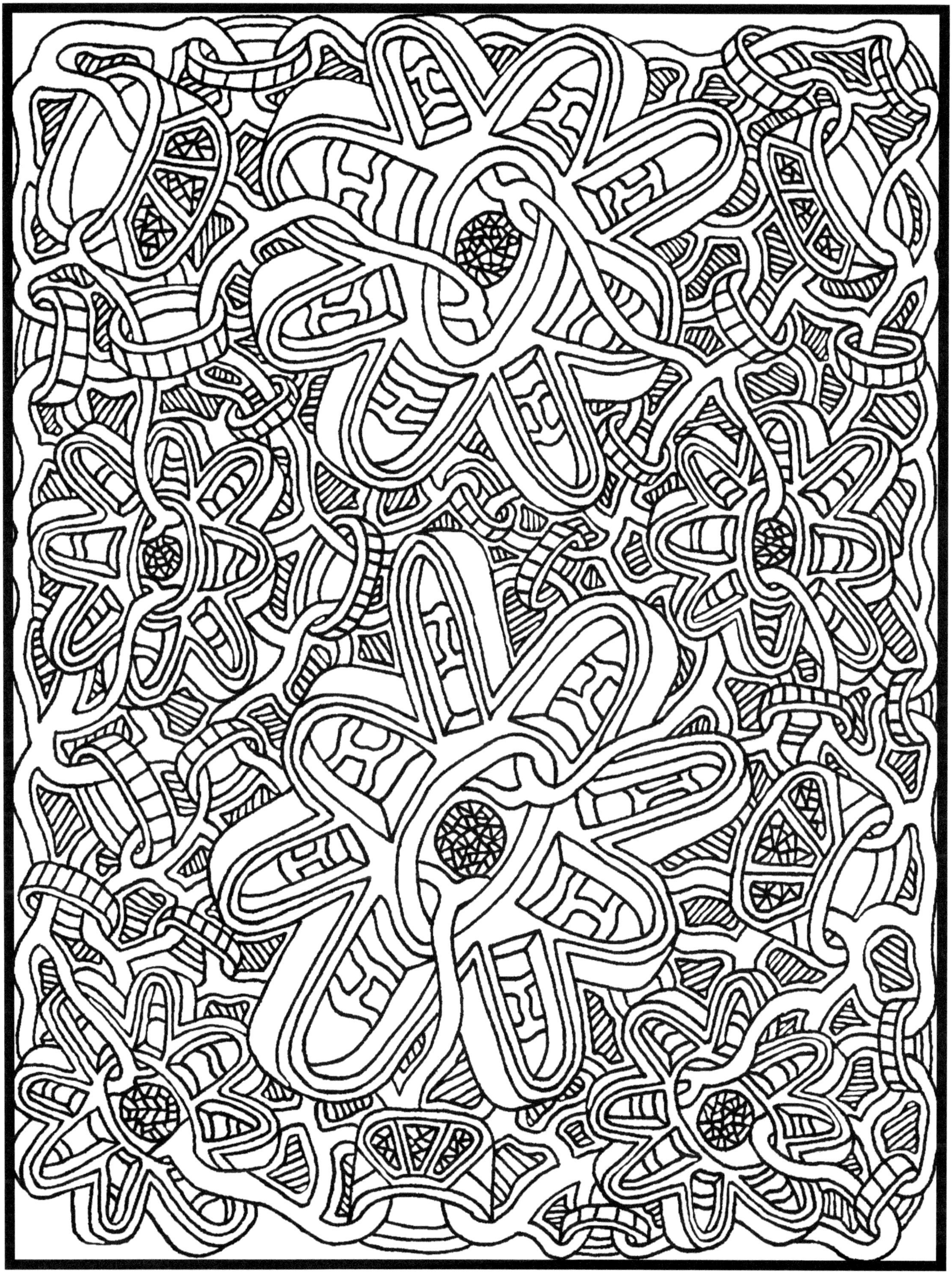

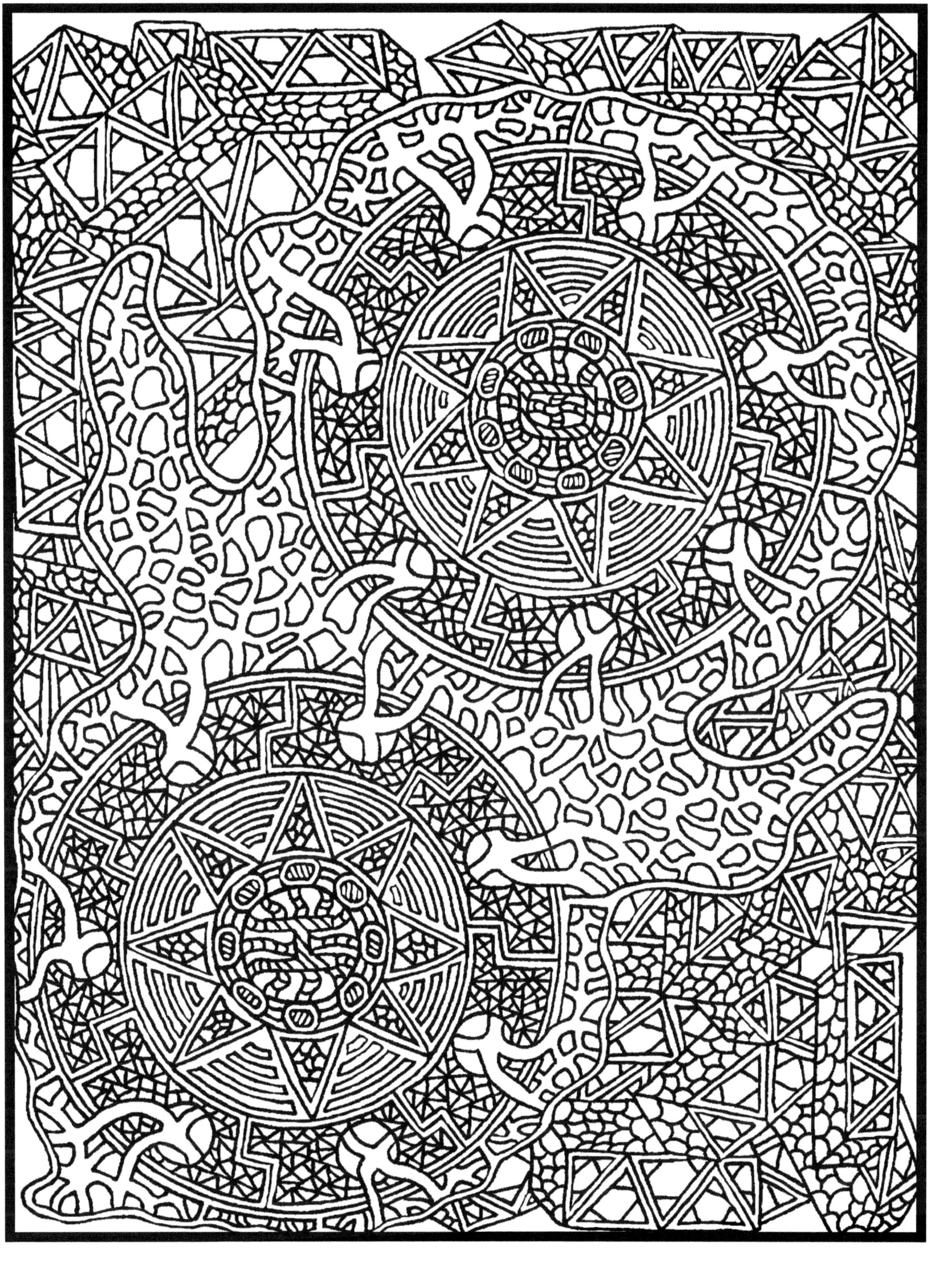

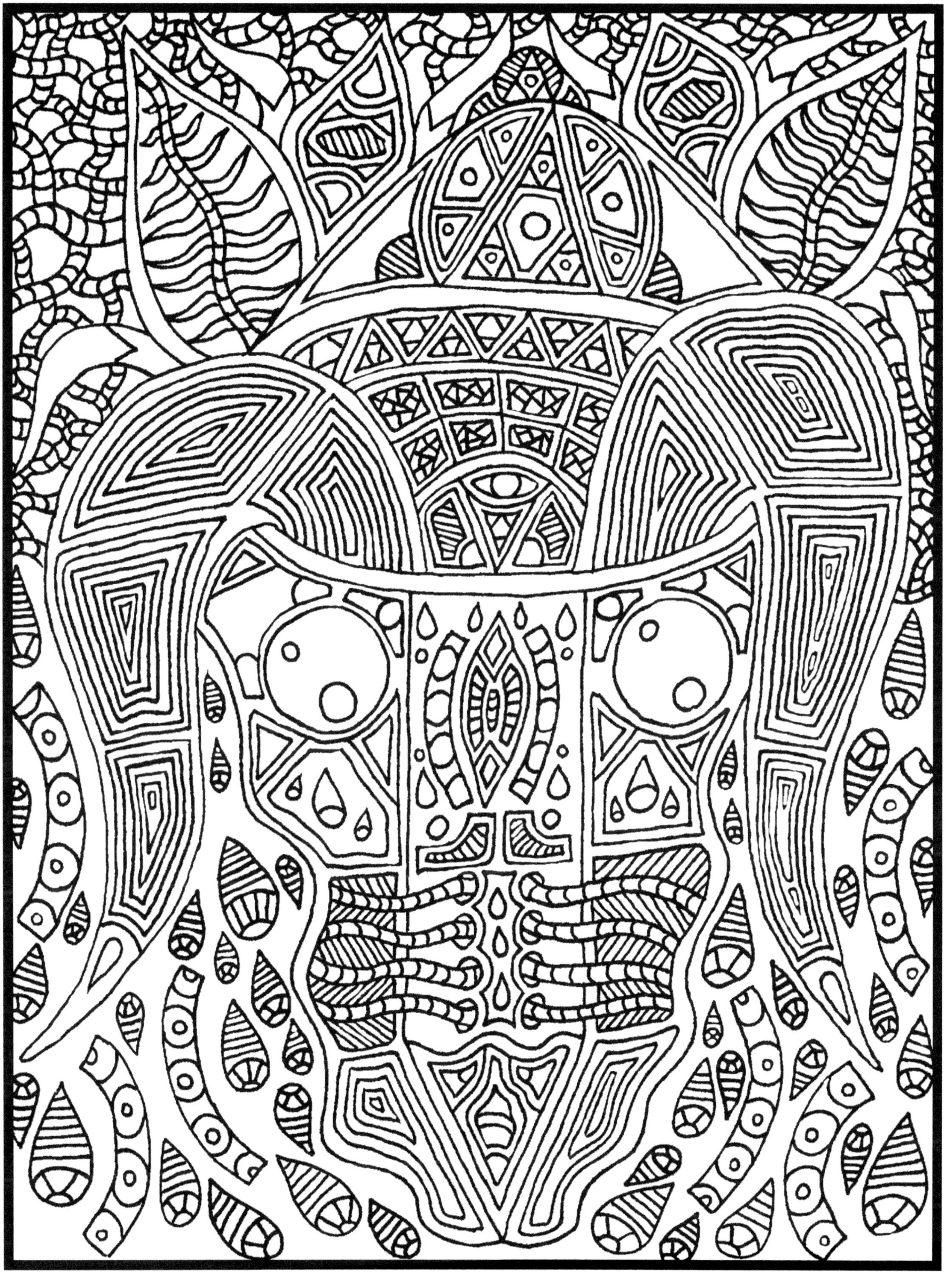

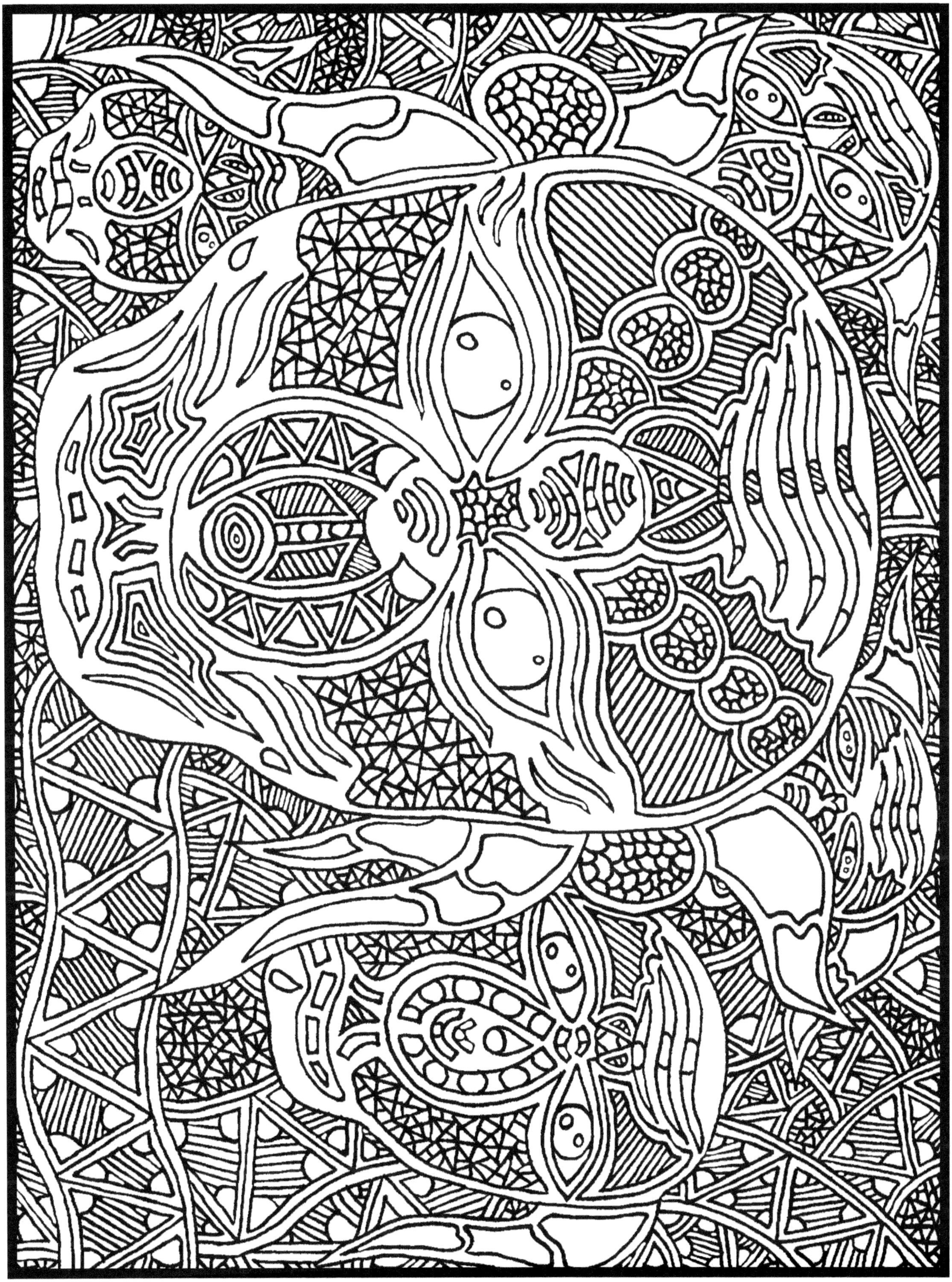

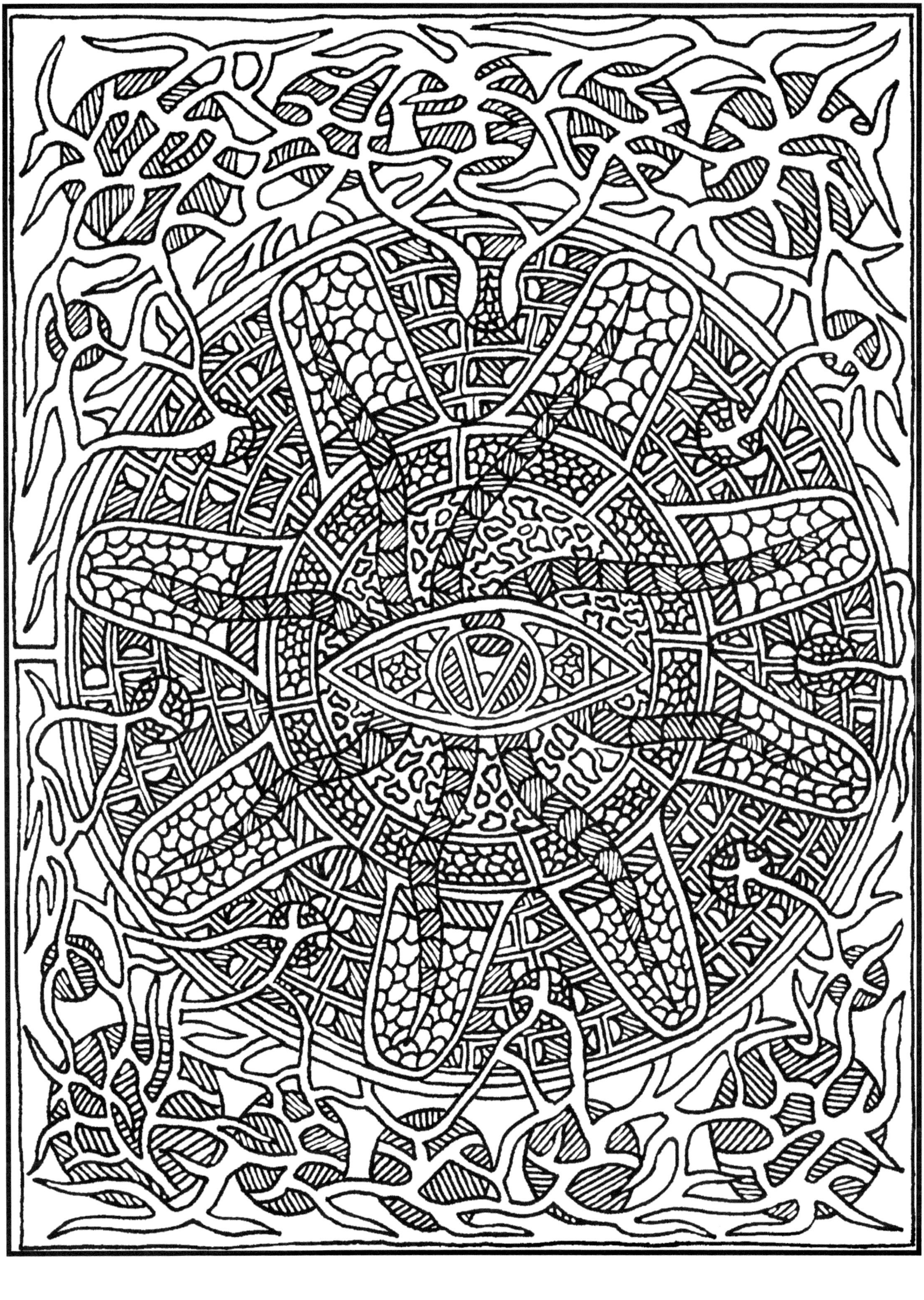

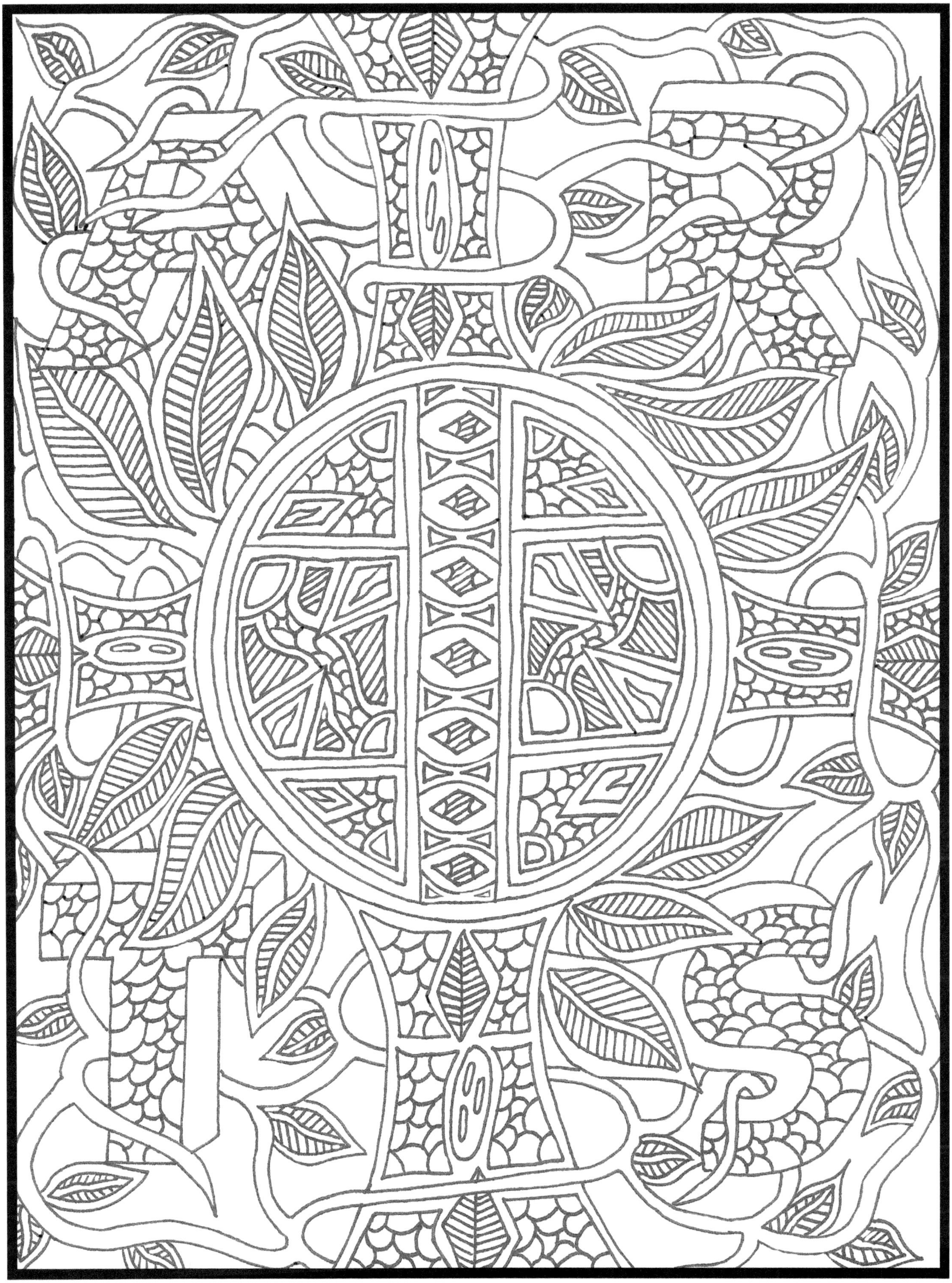

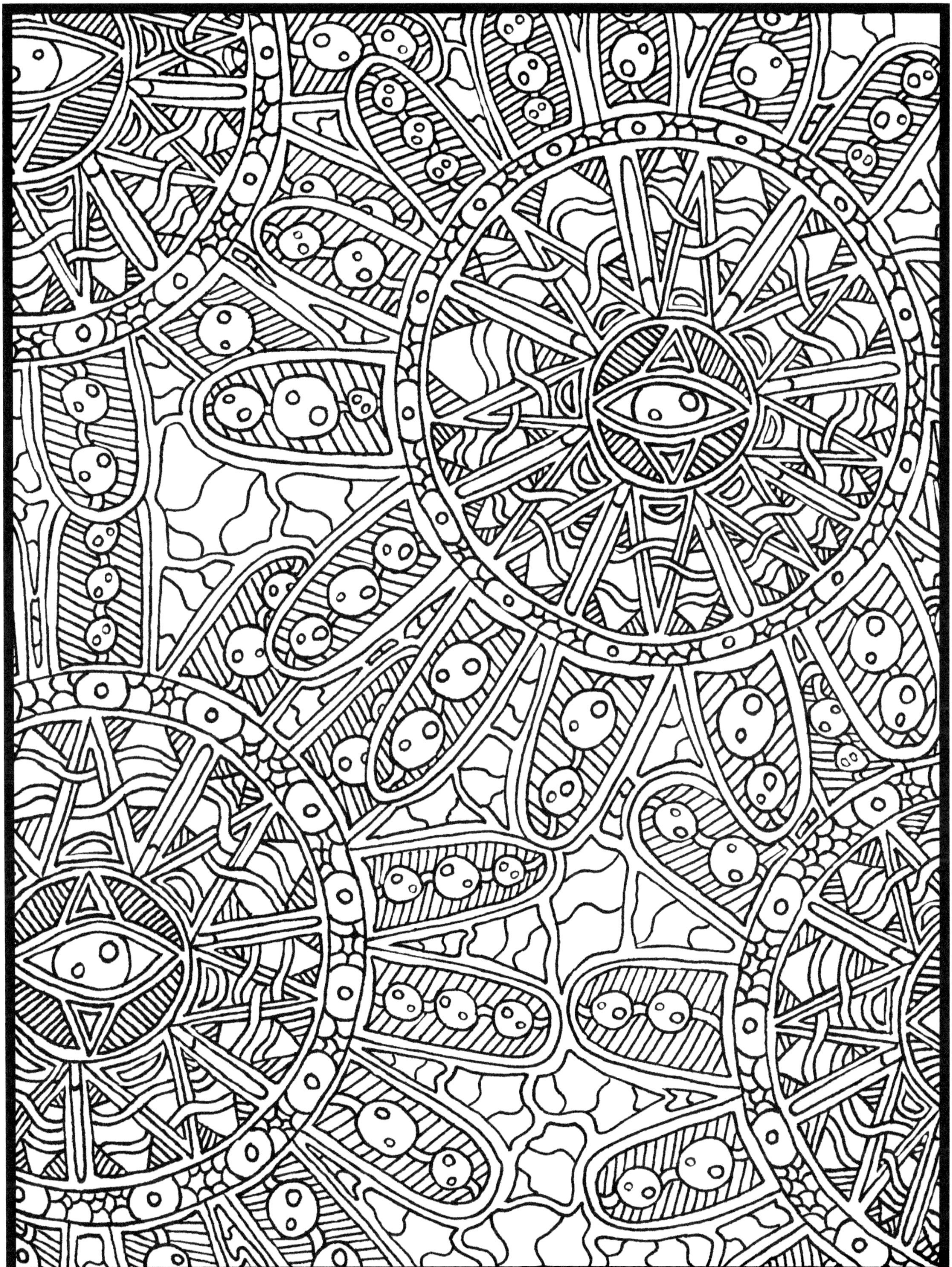

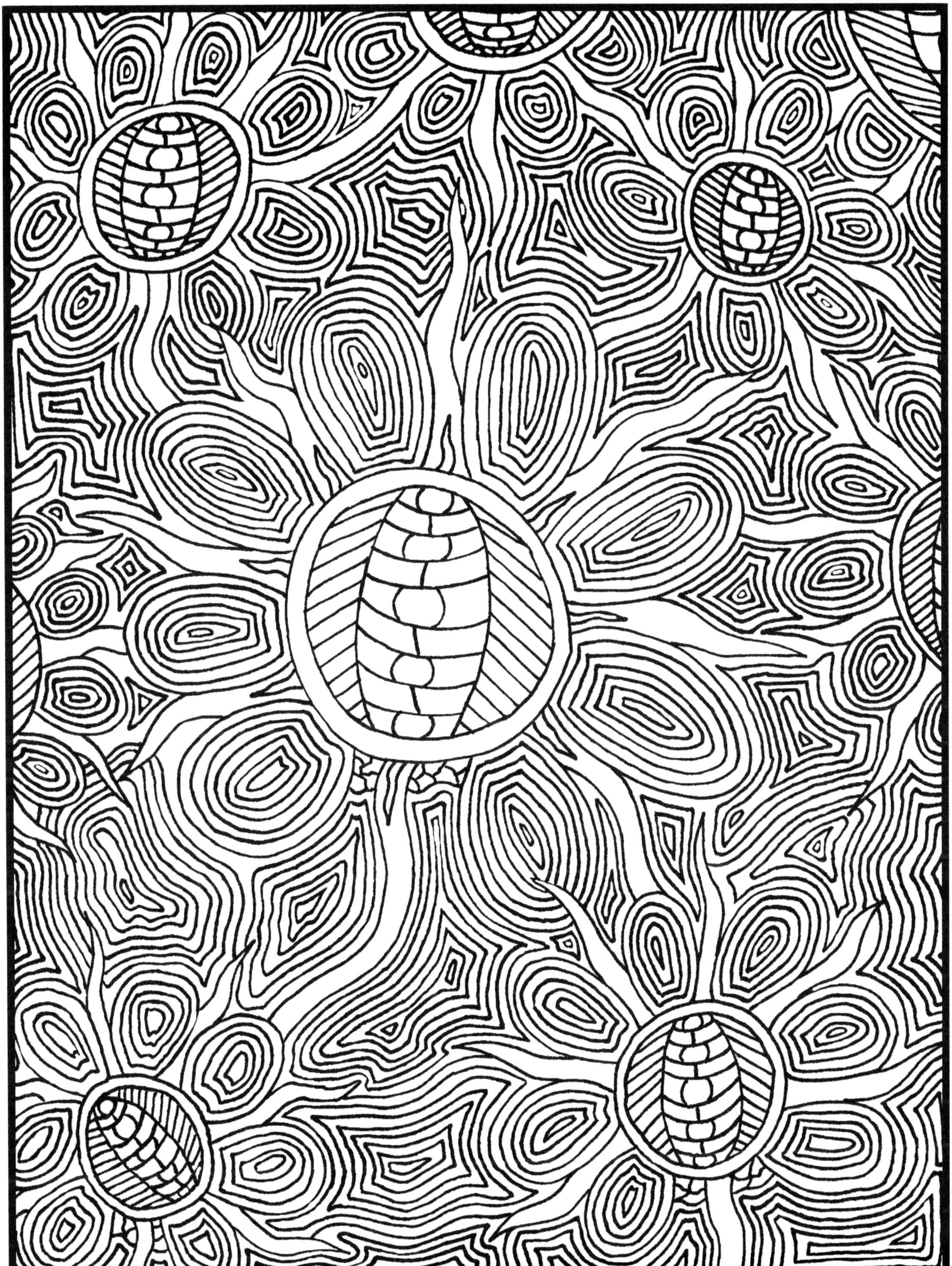

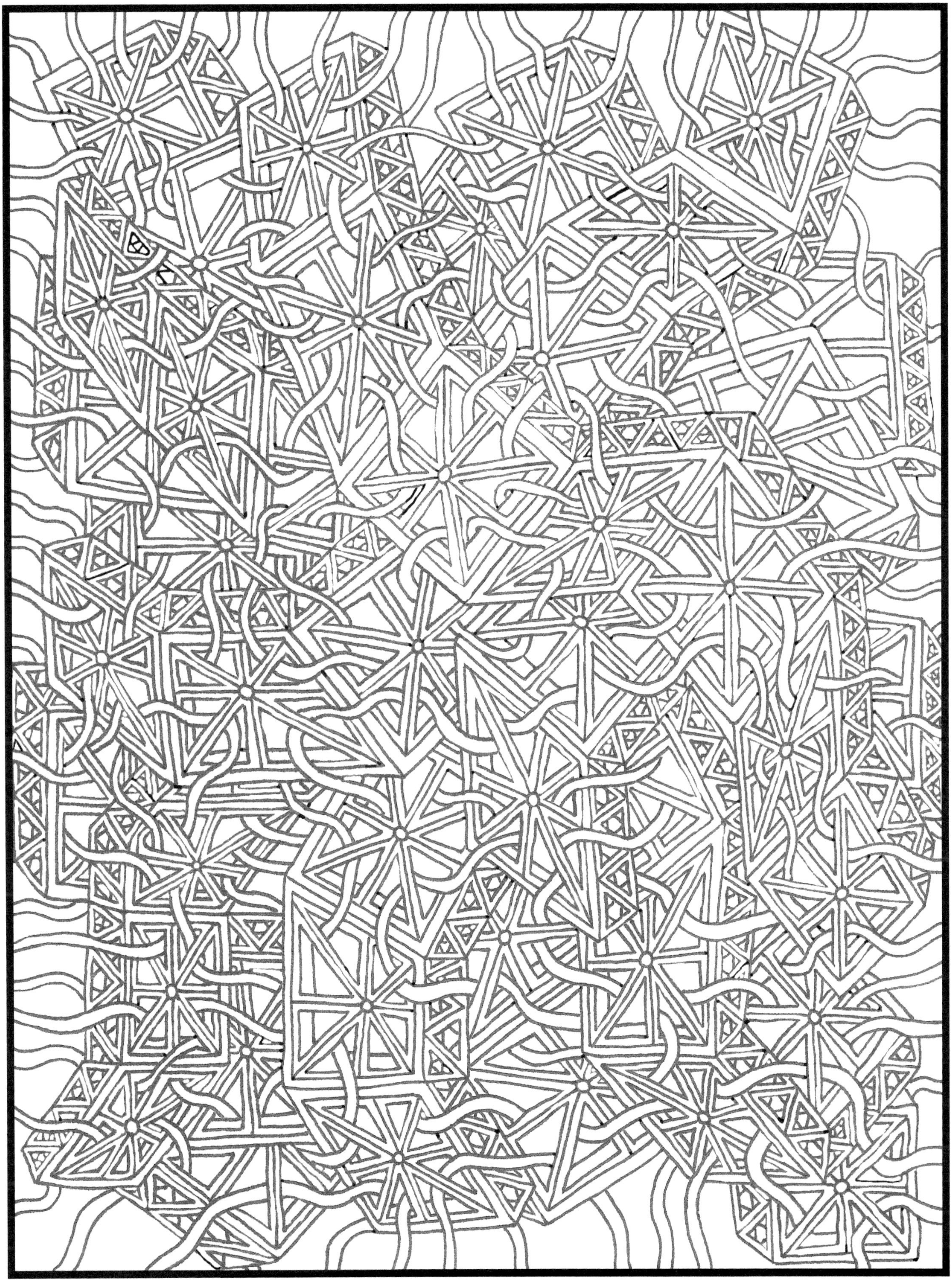

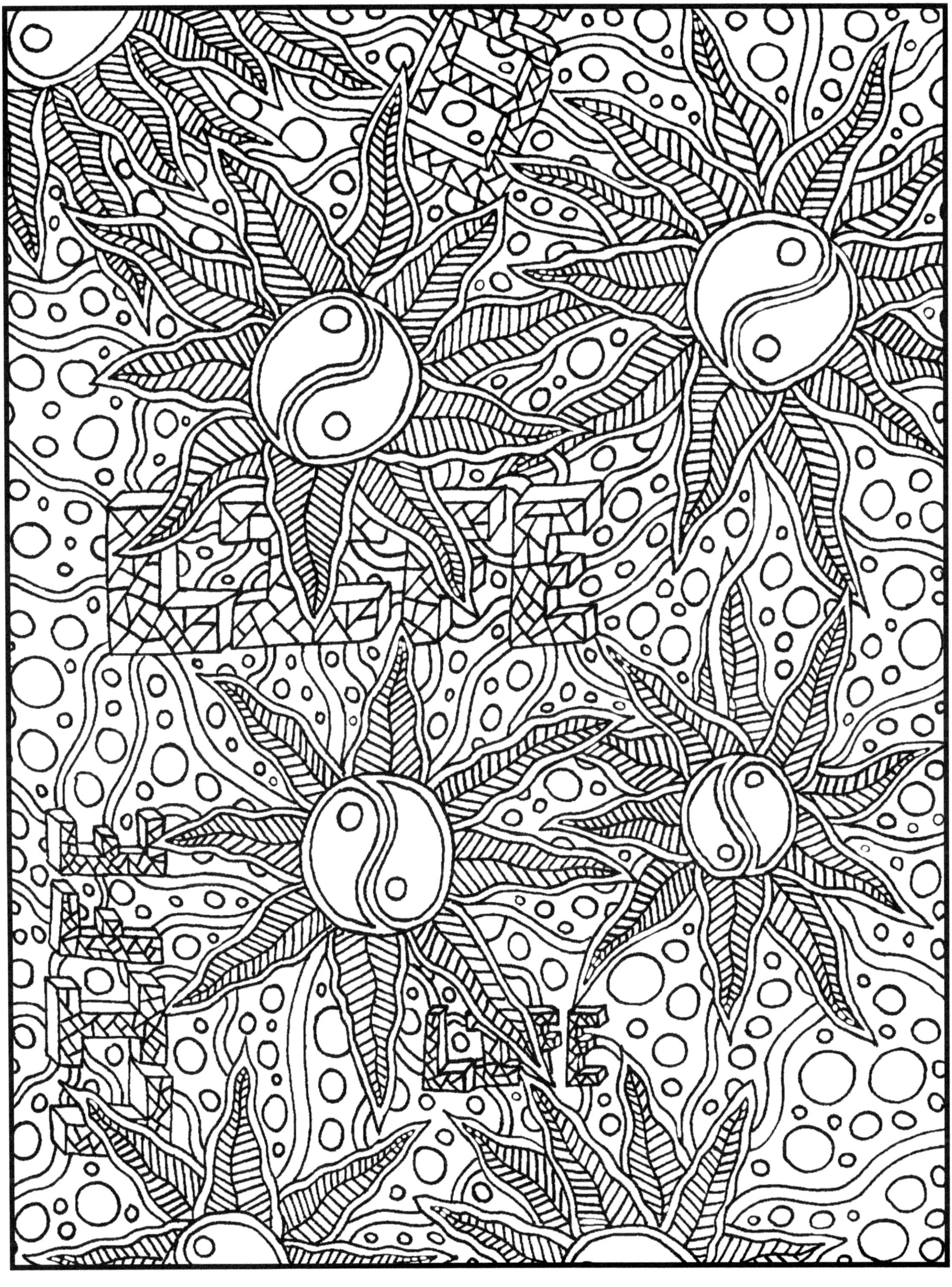

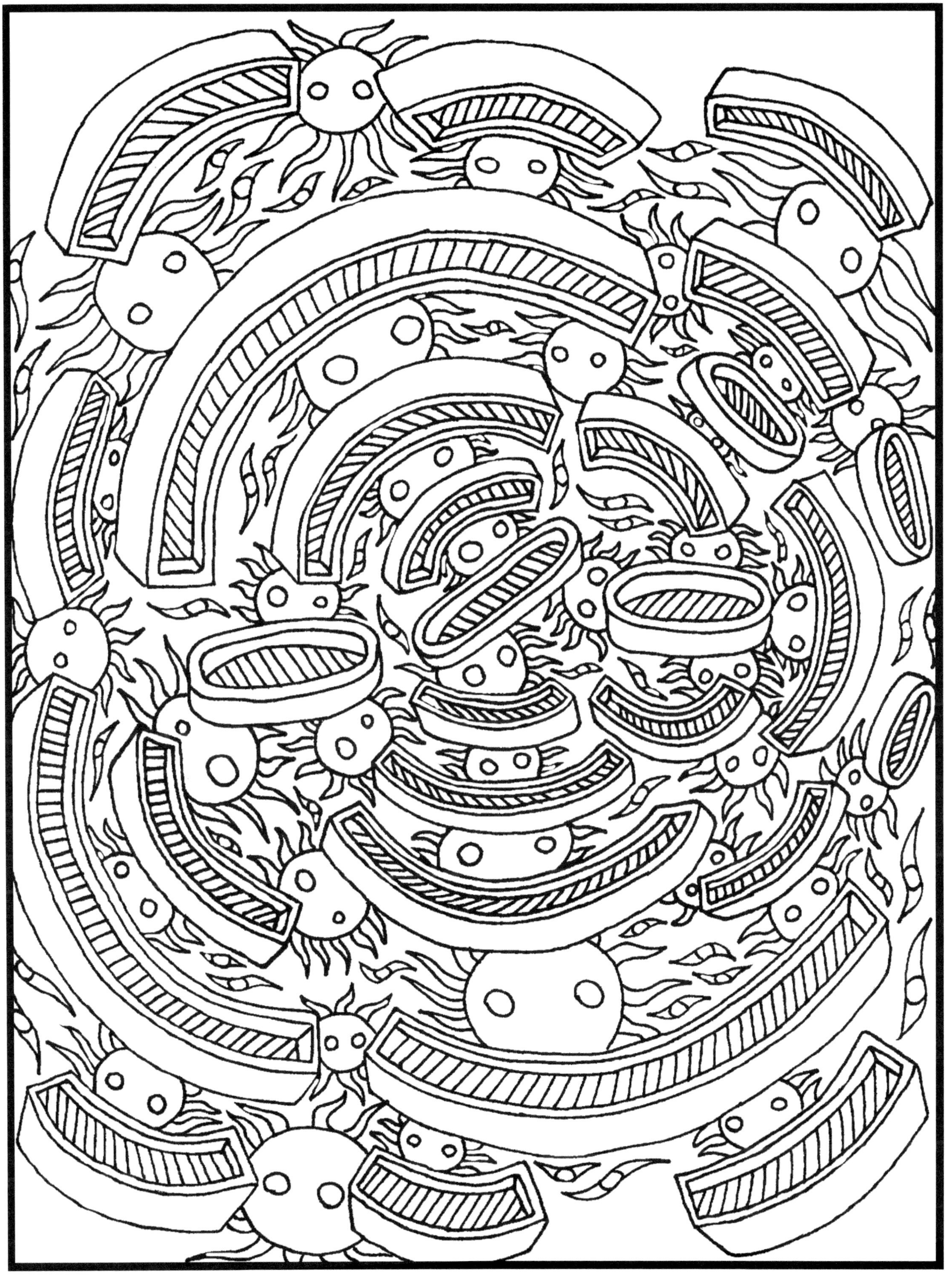

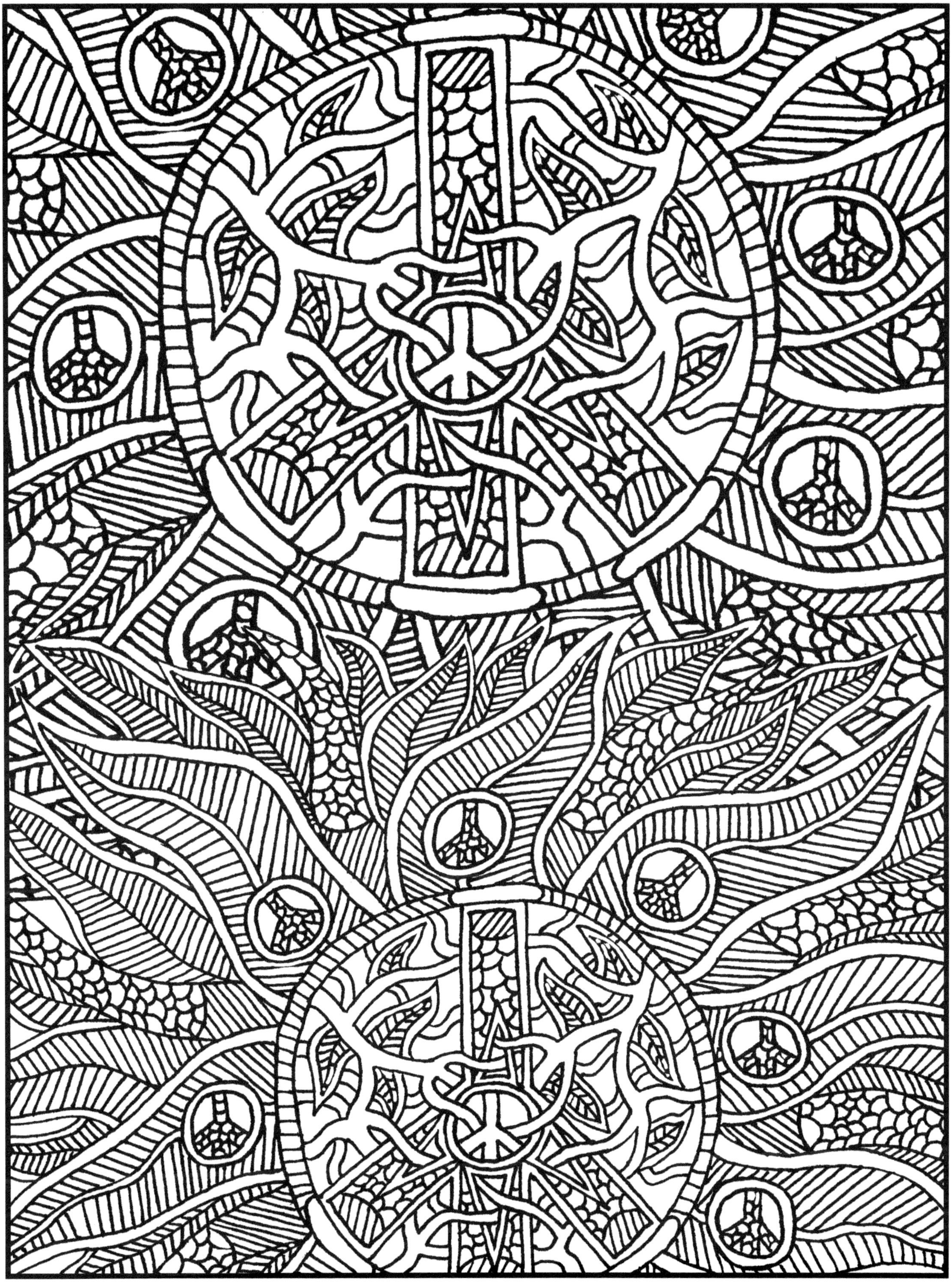

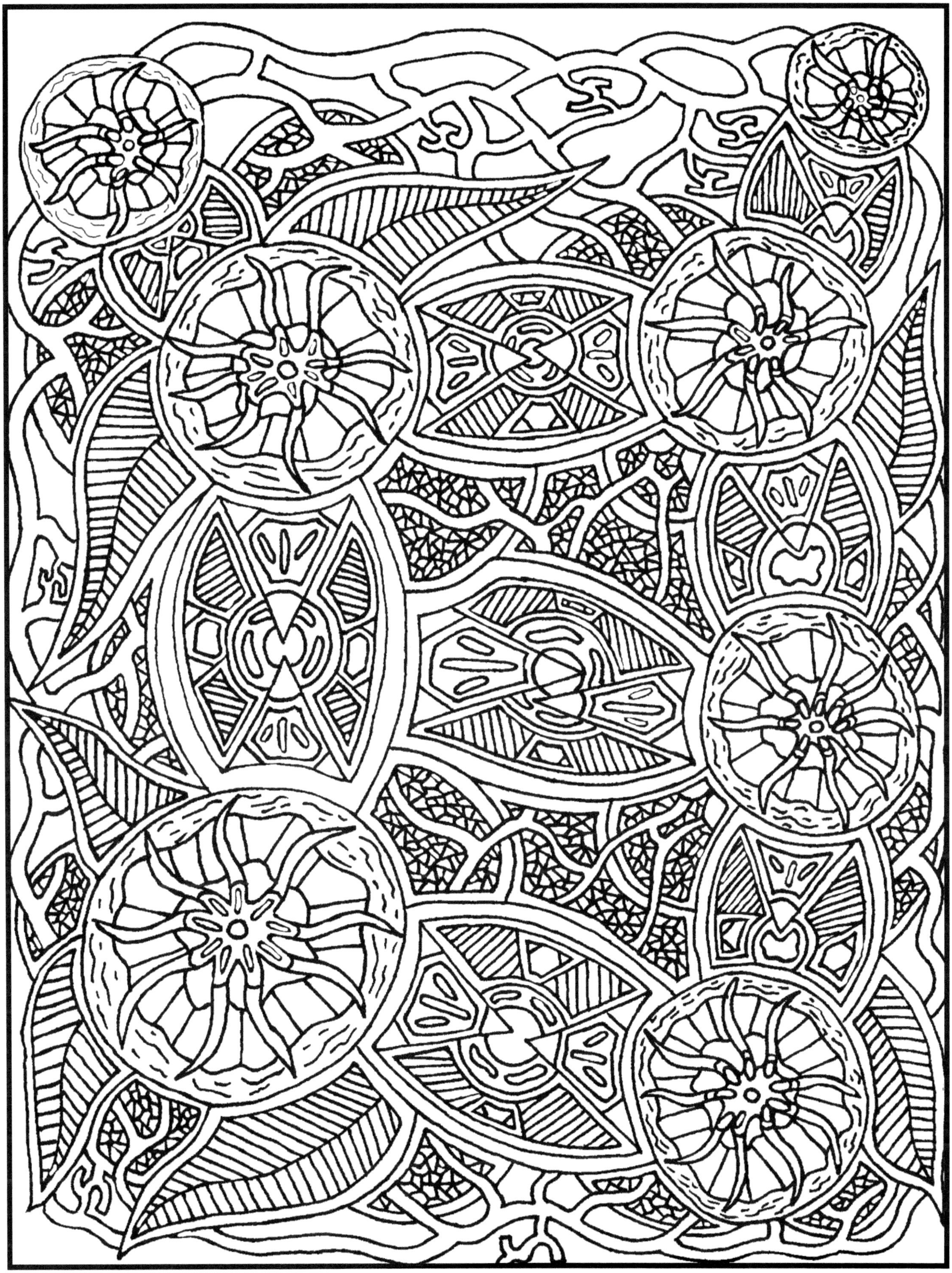

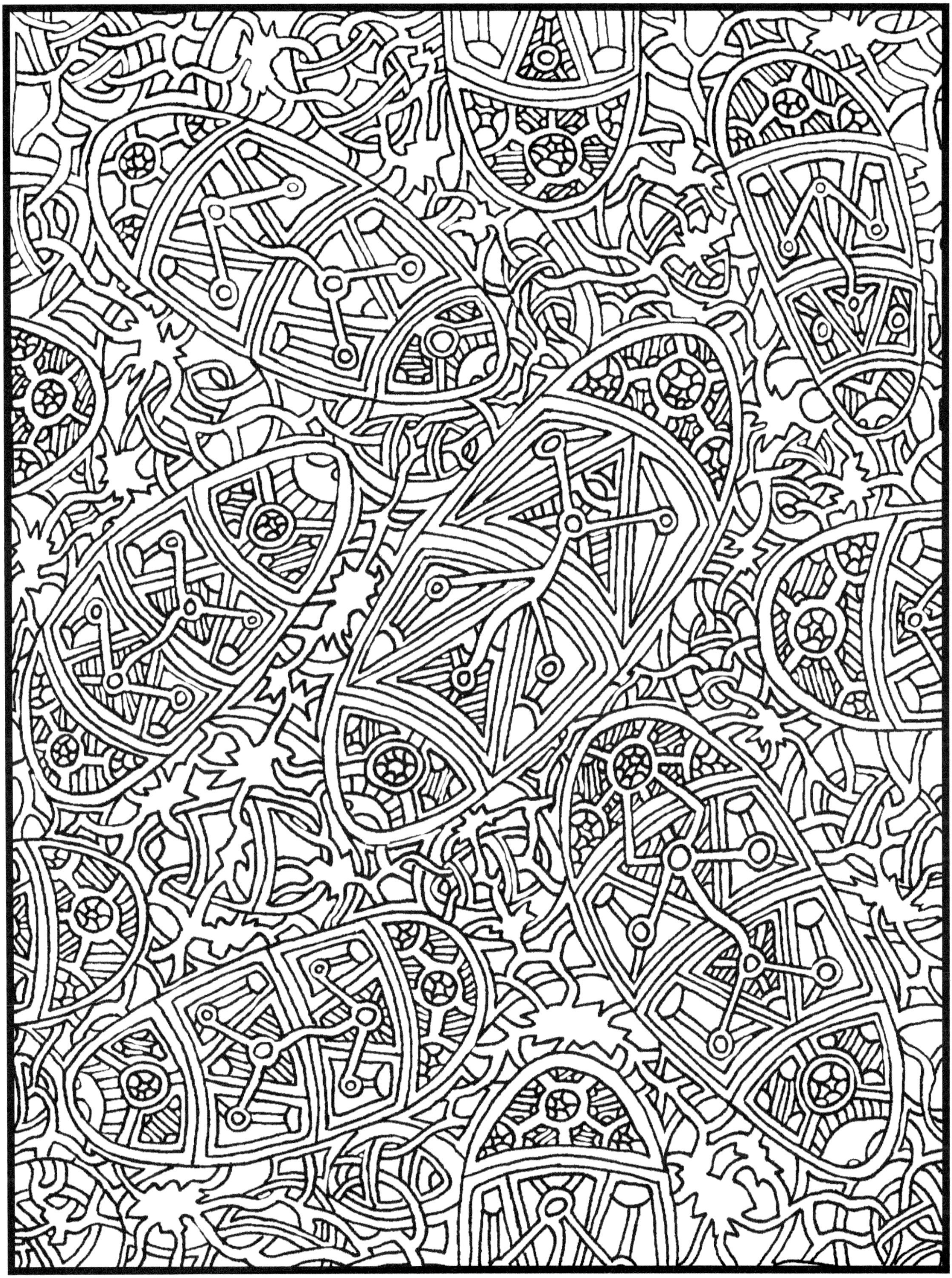

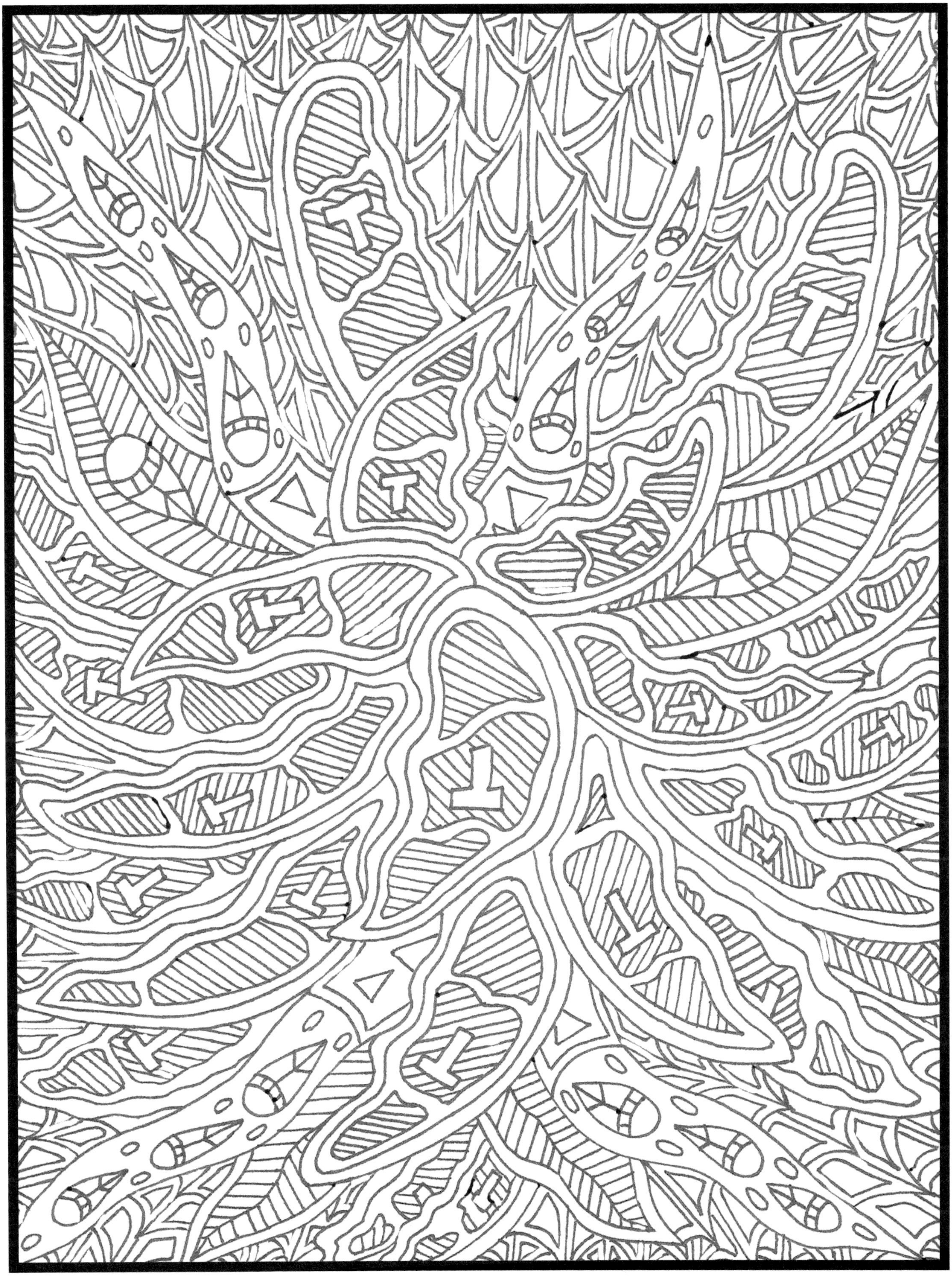

For more books

email me at damonehe@yahoo.com

or mail me at PO. box

2433 Newport Oregon

97365

or you can visit damonesart.com

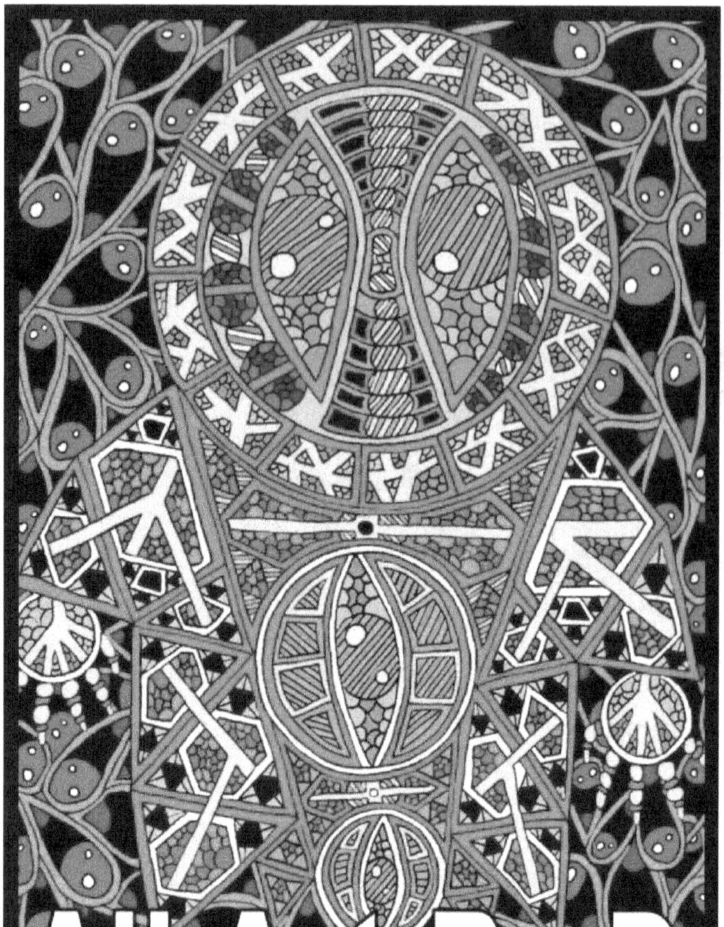

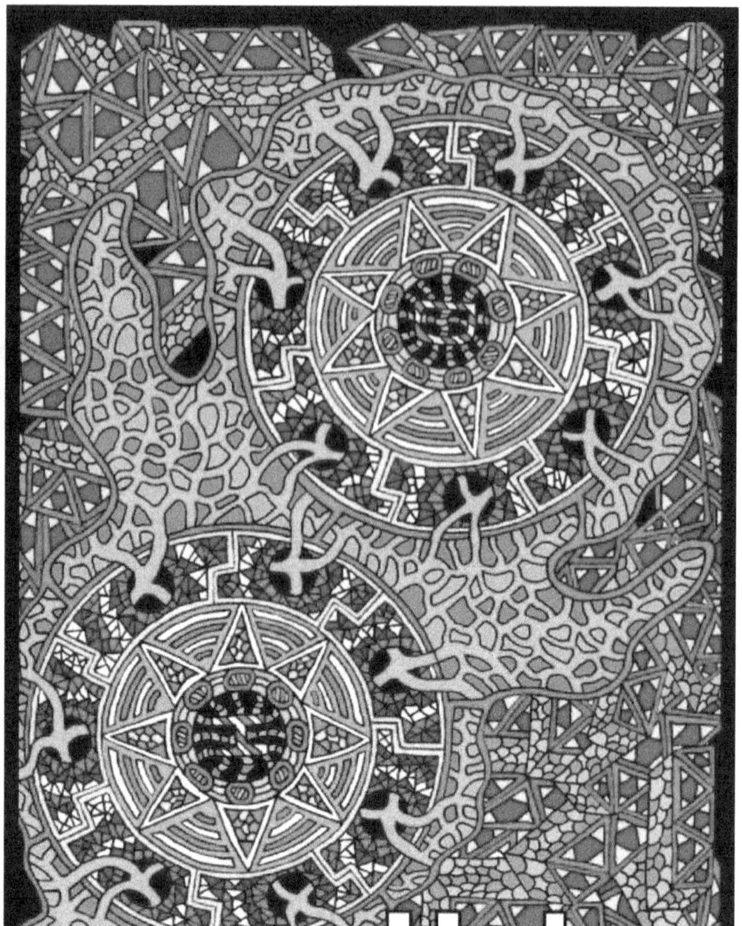

All Art By Damone Heins

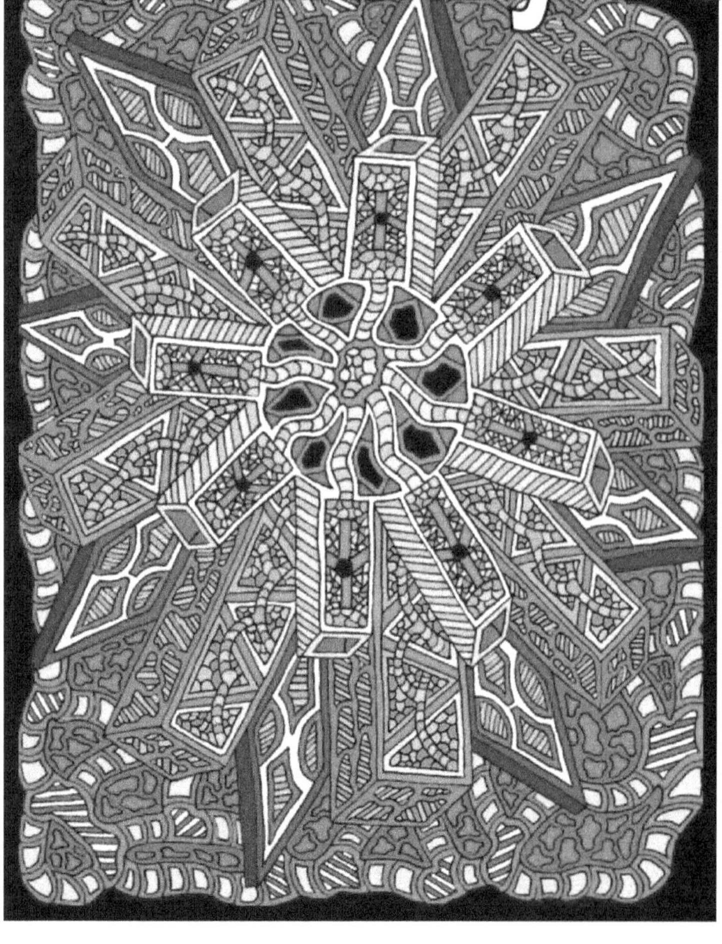

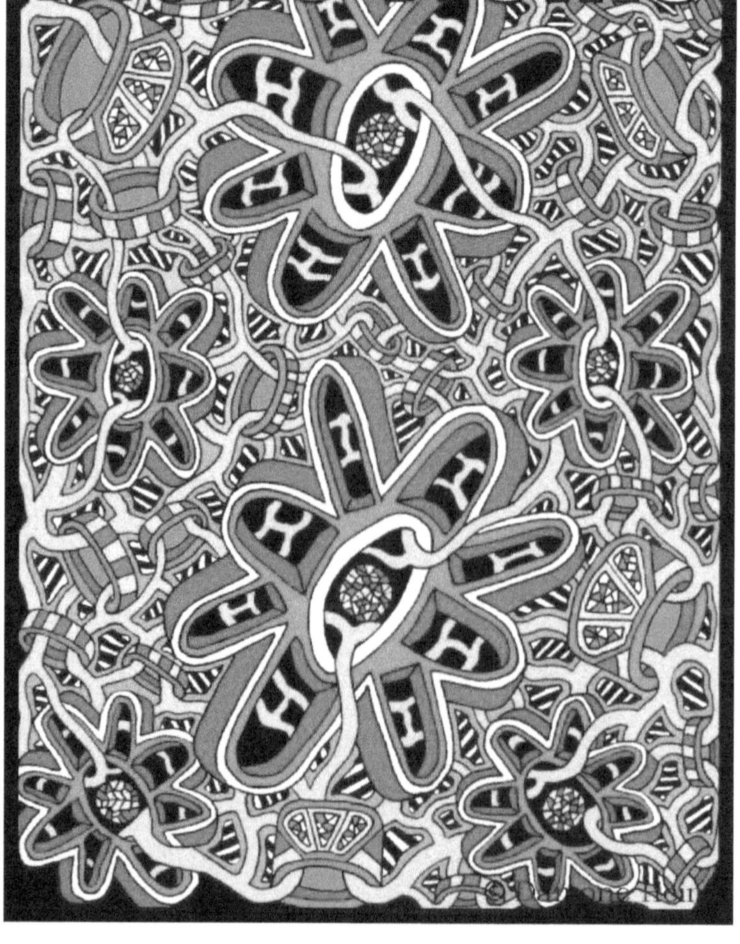

www.ingramcontent.com/pod-product-compliance
Lightning Source LLC
Chambersburg PA
CBHW080541190526
45169CB00007B/2593
9781533106797